By the same Author

Walk in the beautiful Conwy Valley (5 editions)

Walk in magnificent Snowdonia (3 editions)

Snowdonia: ancient trackways
              Roman roads
              packhorse trails

to Sam, Joe

Walk

in the

Vale of Ffestiniog

Ralph Maddern

FOCUS PUBLICATIONS · WINDSOR

© Ralph Maddern

First published in Great Britain 1986

Focus Publications
9 Priors Road
Windsor
Berkshire SL4 4PD

ISBN 0 9505053 6 6

Printed in Great Britain by
David Green Printers Ltd, Kettering,
Northamptonshire.

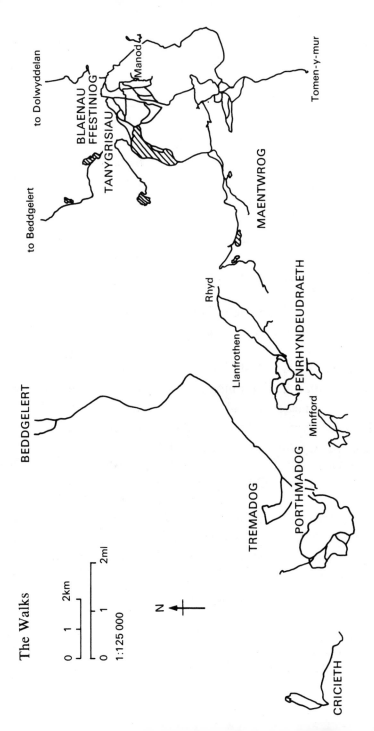

The Walks

0 1 2km
0 1 2ml
1:125 000

N

BEDDGELERT

to Beddgelert

to Dolwyddelan

BLAENAU
FFESTINIOG

TANYGRISIAU

Manod

Tomen-y-mur

MAENTWROG

Rhyd

Llanfrothen

PENRHYNDEUDRAETH

Minfford

TREMADOG

PORTHMADOG

CRICIETH

Contents

Illustrations

by

Mair Perring

Outline Portraits

Compass and Country Code

When walking in areas away from habitation it is highly desirable, if not essential, to use a compass which can at least ensure that everyone knows when one is going in the wrong direction. Even in inhabited areas a compass bearing is often the most efficient means of finding one's way. Compass bearings appear frequently in the text. Of course, it is possible to find one's way without reference to them but the bearings do ensure that the way is clearly stated. Bearings are given to the nearest 10°.

To use a hand compass hold it in a horizontal position and allow the needle to steady. Bring the needle's north pointer into coincidence with north (N) which is 0° or 360°. The direction of a bearing may then be determined.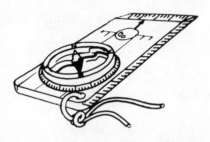

These walks offer views as splendid as may be encountered anywhere. All is free for the enjoyment of walkers but everyone using the walks is asked to keep to the route described and adhere to the Country Code which may be summarized as follows.

Avoid: damaging crops, trees, hedges, fences or walls,
       disturbing farm animals,
       dropping lighted matches or cigarette ends,
       fouling pools or streams,
       digging up wild flowers,
       robbing birds' nests.

Keep dogs under control. (Better still, leave your dog at home. The Vale of Ffestiniog is a sheep-grazing country. Sheep should not be disturbed, least of all in the lambing season).

Close all gates except those intended to be left open.

Clear up all litter including glass.

Welsh

Place names in Welsh are fascinating because of the descriptions they offer of their locations. That is why interpretations are given where this is possible. Understanding what the name means is often a major clue to knowing the place itself. Pronunciation can be quite difficult for a non-Welsh speaker but it is worth trying to get the right sound. The main sounds, where these differ from English, are set out below.

a	as in *are*
c	always hard as in *car*
Ch	as in the Scottish *loch*
e	'ay' as in say
f	as in the English 'v'
Ff	as in the English '*f*'
g	always hard as in *give*
Ll	place the tongue to form 'l' but emit a passage of air through the tongue to merge with the following letter
r	rolled more strongly than in English
Rh	both the 'r' and the 'h' are pronounced
Th	'th' as in *both*
Dd	also 'th' but as in *this*
u	'i' as in *it* or '*ee*' as in *feet*
w	'oo' as in *roost* (Llanrwst = Llanroost) — it also works like the English 'w'
y	'u' as in *fun* or '*ee*' as in *feet* or 'i' as in *pin* (you have to listen)

J, K, Q, V, X and Z do not appear in Welsh as these sounds are conveyed by other letters or dipthongs.

The term *critch-cratch* is much used in the text. It refers to a gate, hung in a U or V-shaped enclosure, which is sometimes known as a 'kissing gate'. *Critch-cratch* seems much more illustrative and evocative.

YOUR RIGHTS OF WAY ARE
Public footpaths — on foot only. *Sometimes waymarked in yellow*
Bridleways — on foot, horseback and pedal cycle. *Sometimes waymarked in blue*
Byways (usually old roads), most 'Roads Used as Public Paths' and, of course, public roads — all traffic.
Use maps, signs and waymarks. Ordnance Survey Pathfinder and Landranger maps show most public rights of way.

ON RIGHTS OF WAY YOU CAN
Take a pram, pushchair or wheelchair if practicable
Take a dog (on a lead or under close control)
Take a short route round an illegal obstruction or remove it sufficiently to get past.

YOU HAVE A RIGHT TO GO FOR RECREATION TO
Public parks and open spaces — on foot
Most commons near older towns and cities — on foot and sometimes on horseback
Private land where the owner has a formal agreement with the local authority

IN ADDITION you can *use* by local or established *custom or consent,* but ask for advice if you're unsure:
Many areas of open country like moorland, fell and coastal areas, especially those of the National Trust, and some commons
Some woods and forests, especially those owned by the Forestry Commission
Country Parks and picnic sites
Most beaches
Canal towpaths
Some private paths and tracks.
Consent sometimes extends to riding horses and pedal cycles.

FOR YOUR INFORMATION

County councils and London boroughs maintain and record rights of way, and register commons.
Obstructions, dangerous animals, harassment and misleading signs on rights of way are illegal and you should report them to the county council
Paths across fields can be ploughed, but must normally be reinstated within two weeks
Landowners can require you to leave land to which you have no right of access
Motor vehicles are normally permitted only on roads, byways and some 'Roads Used as Public Paths'
Follow any local bylaws

AND, WHEREVER YOU GO, FOLLOW THE COUNTRY CODE

Enjoy the countryside and respect its life and work
Guard against all risk of fire
Fasten all gates
Keep your dogs under close control
Keep to public paths across farmland
Use gates and stiles to cross fences, hedges and walls
Leave livestock, crops and machinery alone
Take your litter home
Help to keep all water clean
Protect wildlife, plants and trees
Take special care on country roads
Make no unnecessary noise.

This Charter is for practical guidance in England and Wales only.

Published with financial support from the

BLAENAU FFESTINIOG

WONDROUS SENSATIONS

To experience them one should launch out at the head of the Vale where trickling streams coalesce into gushing rivulets converging to form silky waterfalls of virgin purity yet untainted by the world downstream. In Blaenau the secret is to make for a height : any one will do for a beginning. Some heights are within the town; others are part of the grand sculpture of magnificent mountainous landscape.

If the sky is disgorging a flood, if a steam locomotive adds its smoke to plumes from coal fires, then we are fortunate in having an opportunity to imbibe an atmosphere representing the traditional Blaenau when men trudged to work on wet winter mornings, and back home in the evenings after spending the day at a quarry face. The product they produced satisfied a commercial need when Britain's towns were rapidly expanding. If that were the sole purpose of this place the community would have died when the market found it could satisfy demand for roofing slates with a cheaper, artificial product. Across the world are ghost towns that boomed then shrank to skeletons because nothing could sustain them when the source of their creation was exhausted.

No ghost stalks here. Here, industrialism was a catalyst : an agent that concentrated inherent cultural characteristics of the community it created. When the catalyst was withdrawn the community was shaken but something of enduring structure remained. Our purpose now is to discover its quality. To begin within the town itself.

Walk 1.   Distance : 3.2km, 2ml.

From the Blaenau PO (0.0km; elevation 244m, 800ft) walk NW along the A470 for 500m and turn left to the hump-backed bridge that spans the railway. If the steam train is on its way up the Vale this bridge offers an opportunity for an authentic taste of old Blaenau as the locomotive passes beneath to the station.

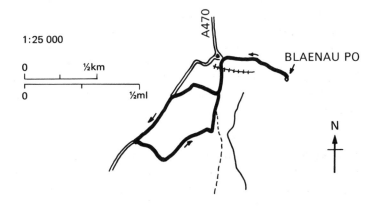

Continue past the square to the second turning right, along that street to the end, turn left then fork right along a tarmac path to the B4414 (1.1km), SW along the road for 300m, turn left onto a quarry road to a gate on the left (1.6km), bear NE and E to a gate and then a fence opening (2.0km). SE is a mound from which to view the valley and town.

If you are carrying a cassette recorder with head phones, or if your memory is sufficiently primed, this would be a place — standing above the town yet almost in it — to switch on *Côr Meibon y Brythoniaid,* or *Côr Meibion y Moelwyn,* or *The Royal Oakley Silver Band.* All have two essential qualities for continuity : high artistic standards attained through dedication, and a capacity for adapting to changing conditions.

The Royal Oakley Silver Band was formed in the mid-nineteenth century — as "the poor man's introduction to music" — by slate quarrymen who worked from seven in the morning until five in the afternoon. Now, half the band membership are teenagers who benefit from music tuition in schools. They offer a repertoire extending across a spectrum from marches through ballads to classical and modern popular composers. A century of folk memory has led the town to believe that its band will be a regular prize winner at competitions and eisteddfodau. Band membership may. be different from times past but The Royal Oakley's attainments continue to match a long tradition of public expectation.

Côr Meibion y Moelwyn — The Moelwyn Male Voice Choir — is named after Y Moelwyn, that splendid massif standing guard on Blaenau's western frontier.

i.   Oer ei drum, garw'i dremynt — yw erioed
            A'i rug iddo'n emrynt;
         Iach oror praidd a cherrynt
         A'i greigiau'n organnau'r gwynt.

16

Cold its ridge, rugged its state — as always
Wrapped in heather cover;
Lush home of the flock and streams
And its rocks organs of the wind.

You can take your pick from among high quality performances in Latin, Italian, German, English and Welsh : Côr Meibion y Moelwyn has done it all as far from home as Iceland. However, that is not considered to be Côr Moelwyn's greatest accomplishment, an honour bestowed upon a piece of the town's heritage — Rhiw Chapel — immaculately restored as the choir's headquarters where future performances are prepared, honed and polished, a process which visitors are welcome to observe.

At the 1985 National Eisteddfod in Rhyl, Côr Meibion y Moelwyn was awarded a first prize, as was Blaenau's other choir, Côr Meibion y Brythoniaid, a singular tribute to this cradle of choral excellence.

Y Brythoniaid refers to the Britons — The Celtic Britons and their language — a cherished tradition taken on international tours : to Hungary in 1975, to California in 1980, to the Continent in 1986; to various towns in Britain; in appearances on television and radio. From stages of the wider world Y Brythoniaid returns to its twice-weekly rehearsals in Ysgol y Moelwyn, and to give concerts in local chapels and schools. Find one such concert, an entirely Welsh occasion, and you will have made a real discovery. Enjoy the unique treat, recall and savour it on this mound, or on any other height above Blaenau.

Walk 2.   Distance : 3.9km, 2½ml.

On reaching the B4414 (1.1km) from the Blaenau PO as in Walk 1, continue SW along the road for 700m, turn left — SE past the farm cottage *Tynddol* — the house in the meadow — to a fork (2.0km). The left fork (070°) leads to a gate (2.3km) and, as in Walk 1, one rejoins the outward route.

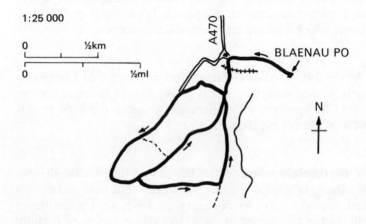

Walk 3.   Distance : 4.5km, 2.8ml.

Beyond the cottage Tynddol, as in Walk 2, take the right fork at 2.0km, bearing 150° right of the fence, veering to E beyond the field wall up onto a mound. Here is another point from which to view the valley and town. Descend the slope to the valley path (2.5km) and turn northward.

Walk 4.   Distance : 6km, 3¾ml.

As in Walk 1 continue along the B4414 (from 1.1km) to a critch-cratch (2.7km), bear E and SE up and around the craggy outcrop known as *Pen-y-cefn* — top of the ridge. Veer NE down to the valley track that bears northward along the floor of the cwm to the town.

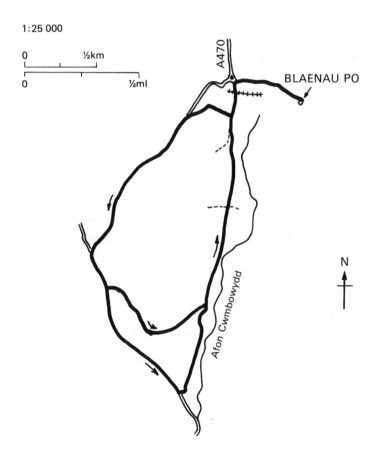

Walk 5.   Distance : 6.5km, 4.1ml.

This route includes the entire length of Cwmbowydd. Follow the B4414 from 1.1km to 3.5km, turn left (E) then northward into the wide valley sheltering within its rugged horizon of ridges.

ii.   Wele rith fel ymyl rhod — o'n cwmpas,
        Campwaith dewin hynod;
      Hen linell bell nad yw'n bod,
      Hen derfyn nad yw'n darfod.

      Behold a guise like an orbit edge — surrounding,
        Masterpiece of a remarkable magician;
      An old distant line that is not in being,
      An old boundary that does not end.

A couple of centuries ago this path along the floor of the cwm was a traditional packhorse trail used by drovers taking herds of animals off to England. Now, it is straddled by Blaenau's re-located sewage works, a feature which one can scarcely fail to appreciate even at a distance.

Skirt left round the sewage works and on to a wall gate (4.6km). There is a path intersection at 4.8km (see Walk 6) and 200m further on we fork right, descending NE to a footbridge (5.1km) spanning a confluence of the Afon Bowydd with a tributary. Up through the woods to the massive rock supporting Blaenau's secondary school (5.4km) and into the town.

Walk 6. Blaenau — Cwmbowydd.
Distance : 1.4km, 0.9ml.

From Blaenau PO (0.0km), turn left (SW) down the adjacent street over the railway and follow the road right, then left, SW past the school into the woods, south and south-eastward to a stile (0.9km) by the Cwmbowydd Farm drive. Turn right (SW) along the farm drive, fork left beyond the gate into the field (1.1km), cross the footbridge SW of the house, continue SW past the barn and W over the wall to join the valley path.

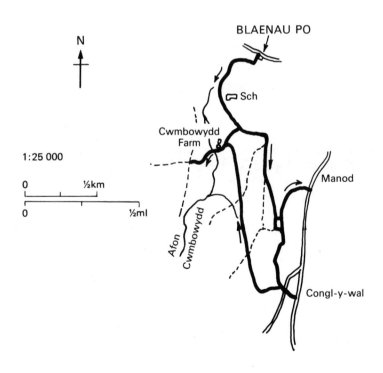

N

BLAENAU PO

Sch

Cwmbowydd
Farm

Manod

1:25 000

0   ½km

0   ½ml

Afon Cwmbowydd

Congl-y-wal

Walk 7.   Blaenau — Manod.
Distance : 2.4km, 1½ml.

As for Walk 6 to the stile by the Cwmbowydd Farm drive (0.9km), turn E along the drive then S (1.1km), take the left fork southward beyond a critch-cratch (1.4km), veer left and continue alongside the railway. Cross the bridge, left (1.9km), and follow the field path to Manod Village, lying at the foot of Manod-bach. (Refer to Walk 10).

Walk 8.   Blaenau — Congl-y-wal — Blaenau.
Distance : 4.9km, 3.1ml.

From the bridge over the railway (1.9km in Walk 7), continue southward to the next bridge (2.0km), turn right and follow the path on 200°, then SE to a stile (2.4km) opposite Congl-y-wal. *Congl* means corner. *Congl-y-wal:* corner of the wall.

If returning to Blaenau, turn right (W), continue past a barn, then northward to a stile (2.8km) and, 100m further on, converge with a path on the left.

Taking the right fork the outward path may be rejoined (3.2km).

Taking the left fork at 2.9km, continue northward through Cwmbowydd Farm to a footbridge (3.9km), through a gated opening to the stile by the farm drive (4.0km), and northward through the woods past the school (4.4km) to the town.

Walk 9.   Blaenau — the Quarries and northward.
Distance : 2.7km, 1.7ml.

From Blaenau PO walk E/SE along the A470 for almost
200m, take the third turning left and continue N, following
the quarry road as it curves eastward between hills of slate
debris. At 1.0km, turn left across the route of an old
tramway and follow the road NW. Before reaching a quarry
building about 500m further on, turn right and maintain a
north bearing beyond the quarry workings to a gate and stile
at the base of Ffridd-y-bwlch (2.4km). Continue uphill on a

bearing of 350°, skirting the corner of a fence, to the left summit (2.7km). Here is a point to see the quarries arranged as a giant artist's model.

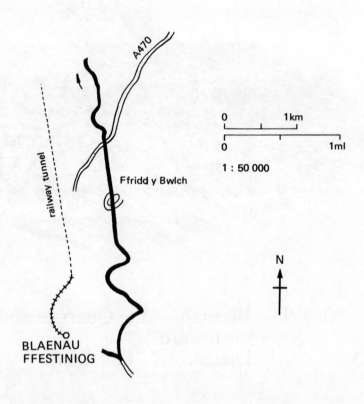

The creators were men working in groups of four: two rockmen who extracted the rock and two men who dressed the rough blocks and split them into usable slates. These groups were dependent upon many others such as surveyors, miners, hauliers, platelayers and machinery attendants. Such a pattern of interdependence is a familiar feature of many mining communities but here in Wales there was a distinct cultural aspect. This can be illustrated by imagining a group of quarry workers taking their midday meal.

A sealed-off section of tunnel converted into *y caban*. Under a *Llywydd,* a chairman, a wide-ranging discussion : on Monday and Tuesday the debate might be about sermons preached in the chapels on Sunday. A good Llywydd sought to have members of his *caban* probe depths of meanings. For the remainder of the week the *caban* might turn to recitation, poetry, choral activities, performances of brass bands. The *caban* also served as a forum for political discussion, and as a cell for organising the North Wales Quarrymen's Union whose stormy history is part of Britain's trade union story.

iii.   Bachgen dengmlwydd gerddodd ryw ben bore,
        Lawer dydd yn ôl, i gwr y gwaith;
    Gobaith fflachiai yn ei lygaid gleision
        Olau dengmlwydd i'r dyfodol maith.

    Cryf oedd calon hen y glas glogwyni,
        Cryfach oedd ei ebill ef a'i ddur;
    Chwyddodd gyfoeth gŵr yr aur a'r faenol
        O'i enillion prin a'i amal gur.

    Neithiwr daeth tri gŵr o'r gwaith yn gynnar;
        Soniwyd am y graig yn torri'n ddwy;
    Dygwyd rhywun tua'r tŷ ar elor,
        Segur fydd y cŷn a'r morthwyl mwy.

    A ten year old boy walked early one morn,
        Many a day ago, to begin work;
    Hope flashed in his blue eyes
        The light of ten years to the vast future.

Strong was the old heart of the blue crags,
   Stronger was his gimlet and steel;
Wealth of the man of gold and manor swelled
   From his meagre earnings and frequent pain.

Last night came three men from the works early,
   Their story was of rock breaking in two;
Someone was brought to the house on a bier,
   Idle will be chisel and hammer from now.

The route northward bears 350° down to the A470 (3.6km,
2.2ml), across the road and along wheeltracks passing Moel
Dyrnogydd on the left and on to Dolwyddelan (14.5km,
9.1ml) as described in **Walk in Magnificent Snowdonia**.

Walk 10   Blaenau — Manod-bach
summit.
Distance : 1.9km, 1.2ml.

From the Blaenau PO walk E/SE along the A470 for 300m,
fork left at the fifth turning left and continue round the
massive boulder formation onto a path that winds up to a
lane (0.4km). Turn right, follow the lane, bearing 150°, to a
path (0.5km) and on to a T-junction opposite a row of
terraced cottages (0.8km). Turn right and continue to the site
of an old woollen mill (1.0km).

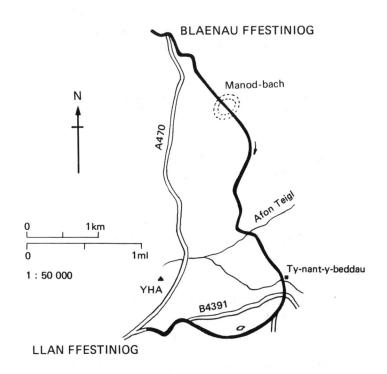

BLAENAU FFESTINIOG

Manod-bach

N

A470

Afon Teigl

0   1km

0   1ml

1 : 50 000

Ty-nant-y-beddau

▲
YHA

B4391

LLAN FFESTINIOG

Stand on the little stone bridge awhile. If Blaenau's weather has been living up to its reputation feel the massive power which this mill used to harness, tumbling down from Manod-bach that rocky mass looming skywards.

Turn left along the path by the bridge and begin the climb. Mark a point with the eye on the summit ridge, general bearing 140°, and continue across the old tramway track to the summit (elevation 473m, 1550ft).

A splendid viewpoint. To the east is the larger Manod-mawr, and between the two is Llyn y Manod, the Manod lake, a peaceful retreat for anglers. To the south-west is Llan Ffestiniog and, facing us across the valley to the west, the Moelwyns, those two solid sentinels which a bard once transformed.

27

iv.   Gwnaeth Duw'r ddau Foelwyn, meddant i mi,
        O garreg nad oes ei chadarnach hi.

        Ond wrth syllu arnynt ambell awr
        Ar fore o wanwyn, amheuaf yn fawr

        Mai o bapur sidan y torrodd o
        Y ddau ohonynt ymhell cyn co',

        A'u pastio'n sownd ar yr wybren glir
        Rhag i'r awel eu chwythu ar draws y tir.

        God made both Moelwyns, I am told,
        From the strongest stone.

        But gazing at them through a carefree hour
        On a spring morning, I doubt it greatly

        From silk paper he cut both
        Long before memory,

        And pasted them securely on the clear sky
        So the breeze does not blow them across the land.

If we are not returning to Blaenau our attention must be
turned southward to Llan, the original Ffestiniog, a retreat
in the heart of the heartland, a sanctuary for the embattled
rebel.

Walk 11. Manod-bach summit — Llan Ffestiniog.
Distance : 6.1km, 3.8ml.

Descend on 140°, cross a stream and join a path from Llyn y Manod at a wall gate. Continue alongside a wall and through an opening 150m further on to a pair of ruins, Bryn-eithin. About 50m beyond the ruins turn left (160°), follow a path across fields to wheeltracks, turn right (220°) and continue down past the farmhouse, Teiliau-mawr (2.1km). Veer left (SE) from the farmyard, past the house Minafon on the left, across the Afon Teigl to a stile and up the hill to a wall stile. Continue SE, crossing the Afon Nant Llyn-morwynion and passing the farmhouse, Ty-nant-y-beddau, on the left. This is a land of streams!

v. Ffrydiau mân llethrau'r Manod — yn bwrlwm
    I gafn Barlwyd isod;
    Lli' ar rus unlliw yr ôd,
    Êl yn dawel ar dywod.

Small streams from the slopes of Manod — bubbling
    To the trough of Marlwyd below;
    The flow starts the colour of snow,
    Goes quietly on sand.

Continue up hill, across the B4391 to a stile and on, bearing 200°, to a farm road (3.5km). Veer right and follow the road for 200m to a gate on the right where the wheeltracks bear 230°. After passing a small reservoir on the right veer to W and continue to a gated wall opening and wall steps (4.8km). Cross the field (300°) to a barn, follow wheeltracks to a critch-cratch and turn left along the B4391 to Llan Ffestiniog PO.

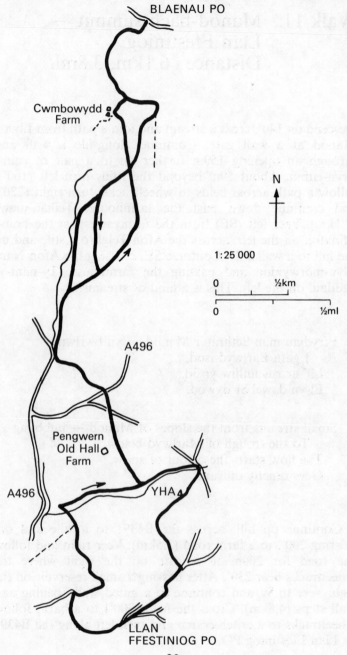

BLAENAU PO

Cwmbowydd
Farm

N

1:25 000

0   ½km

0   ½ml

A496

Pengwern
Old Hall
Farm

A496

YHA

LLAN
FFESTINIOG PO

Walk 12. Valley route to Llan Ffestiniog.
Distance : 6.4km, 4ml.

Follow the route from Blaenau PO described in Walks 6 and 7 to the stile by the Cwmbowydd Farm drive (0.9km). Continue E along the drive for 200m, turn right (S) and take the right fork (SW) via the town's rubbish dump to a gate and stile (1.7km), veer S to SW through woodland up and around the *bryn* (hill), down to the river and along the east side of Afon Cwmbowydd to a stile near the bridge carrying the B4414 (3.3km).

Alternatively — if, for example, the river is running high — veer south from the bryn to a path junction, then SW past the house *Tan-y-bryn* — under the bryn — and southward to the stile near the bridge carrying the B4414 (3.3km).

Turn left to a critch-cratch 50m along the service road, SE and E up the hill to a wall stile (3.7km), down the hill to the A496 (3.9km), across the field to the farm road (4.0km) and on through three gated openings to a farm drive (4.1km).

Llan Ffestiniog may now be seen beyond the farther bryn (160°). Continue past Pengwern Old Hall Farm on the right to a stile on the north side of the Afon Dwyryd (4.7km), turn left (E) to two stiles and waterfalls. Lucky is the walker who sees these falls in full flood — with creaming foam draping ancient boulders, creating little rainbows if the sun should be shining between the leaves.

Then there is an old mill.

vi.   Gweld y melinydd uniaith, ffraeth ei eiriau
        Yn gwynnu yng nghynefin dawch ei hynt.
        Canai wrth ollwng grawn yr haidd a'r gwenith
        I'r gwancus gafn, gan borthi'r meini mâl,
        A'r henfro'n disgwyl am sacheidiau'r fendith
        Tra sychai yntau'r chwŷs o'i lychlyd dâl.

The monoglot miller, witty in language
Whitening in his hazy environment.
He sings while feeding grains of barley and wheat
Into the trough and between the grinding stones,
And the district waiting for sacks of blessing
As he wipes sweat from his dusty forehead.

Turn right and right again over the bridge that spans the river, follow the track S/SW to the Youth Hostel (5.4km), SW and SE past Blaen-ddol to the A470, cross the road and continue up to the Llan Ffestiniog PO.

FFESTINIOG   *RETREAT   SANCTUARY*
                  SELF-SUFFICIENCY

Penffestin is a mail cap or helmet. *Ffestinio* suggests a need to hurry. Whether one should hurry past this place or to it, avoid it or gain protection from its terrain and climate, may depend upon the point of view. Certainly, invaders have hurried past it : the Yorkists and Lancastrians in 1468 and the Royalists and Roundheads almost two centuries later. For others it offered a safe embrace where an identity could be lost and another found. Here was a world apart : external relations were in the hands of a storekeeper who drove a packhorse to Wrexham twice a year to pick up some oddments that locals could not produce. His return was a landmark in the calendar celebrated at the Pengwern Arms, known then — in the eighteenth century — as *Yr Efail* — the smithy — because it was kept by a blacksmith. Here, one could live within a world in itself : isolated, self-sufficient and, of necessity, self-reliant. Now, it is necessary to depart from the village — immerse oneself amongst the forests, fields, streams — to imbibe the sense of how it felt to be here.

Walk 13. Llan to Blaenau.
Distance : 7.5km, 4.7ml.

From Llan Ffestiniog PO (0.0km; elevation : 183m, 600ft) walk W along the B4391 past The Pengwern Arms to a gate on the right (0.8km), eastward to a critch-cratch (1.0km) then northward through gates (1.1, 1.3, 1.6km) down through woods to a path junction (1.7km). (The path on the left continues south-westward for 800m to the A496 where another path leads to Dduallt : see Walk 18). Northward 150m is a footbridge over the Afon Dwyryd, and 150m further on is a footbridge over a tributary, from which paths westward reach the A496 in about 100m. From the south side of the second footbridge ascend N then eastward onto a ridge that divides two valleys and introduces one to a romantic world of deciduous woodland secreting waterfalls dressed in frilly white foam.

Rejoin the outward path (2.8km), turn left and continue NW. On reaching the stile near the bridge carrying the B4414 (4.3km, 2.7ml), turn northward up the farm drive, veer to the right before reaching the house and continue NE and E up the path to stiles at 4.9km and 5.2km. Further along at the path junction (5.4km), veer northward to Cwmbowydd Farm and the stile at the side of the farm drive (6.6km), up through the woods and into the town.

Walk 14. Llan — Rhaeadr Cynfal (Cynfal Falls).
Distance : 1.3km, 0.8ml.

From Llan PO follow the B4391 SW past the Pengwern Arms for 200m, turn left (150°) to a stile, gate and footbridge (0.5km), a critch-cratch, a wall stile (0.6km), then bear 200° veering to SE and a gate at 1.1km.

Fork right to the sound of flowing water crashing into primeval caverns. The river squeezes through a narrow opening into a three-sided chamber, then down through a narrower opening into a smaller *ystafell* where it seems to disappear beneath massive boulders. Only after climbing up the stone steps does one catch a view of it flowing tranquilly on its way down the Vale.

Taking the left fork at the gate (1.1km) one descends in 200m to a footbridge. No frothy white gems here. The long view upstream — especially if Ffestiniog favours us with one of its grey skies — reveals a spectrum of colour from deep black through a range of browns to amber and fluffy fawn.

If one is returning to Ffestiniog, the town may be entered at its south-eastern end near the railway bridge.

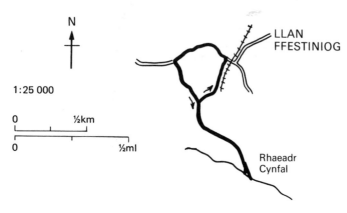

Walk 15.   Rhaeadr Cynfal — Tomen-y-mur.
Distance : 4.4km, 2¾ml.

One walks into a different historical age — back in time nearly 2000 years. From the Cynfal Falls footbridge (0.0km) walk S and SW to stiles at 1.5km, 1.7km and on to the drive of Cynfal-fawr. Veer left to a stile (1.8km) NE of the farmhouse.

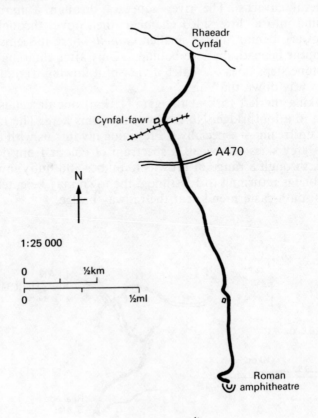

Rhaeadr
Cynfal

Cynfal-fawr

A470

N

1:25 000

0   ½km

0   ½ml

Roman
amphitheatre

Tomen-y-mur

Continue under the railway bridge (1.9km) and southward to two stiles on either side of the A470 (2.2km). South on 160° and a stile over a slate fence (2.9km), 150° to the next stile (3.0km) and continue S alongside the slate fence to a farm drive (3.4km), then to a tarmac road and the site of the Roman amphi-theatre at Tomen-y-mur.

TOMEN-Y-MUR   *PIVOTAL FORT IN ROMAN BRITAIN*

If it were not for the unusual mound, 400m to the SW, one would pass it by as a dip in the ground like any other on the surface of Wales. That 30ft-high mound, or motte, raised by William Rufus — King William II, may have become the site of a castle but for the intervention of Gruffydd ap Cynan (1055–1137), ruling prince of Gwynedd, who drove William back to Chester in the winter of 1095, thereby securing for Wales almost two centuries of independence. Gruffydd was a guerrilla fighter who used tactics of ambush, dispersion, concentration, surprise in conditions of a Welsh winter with masterly effect. William was a strategist who sought to complete England's conquest of the British land mass, eliminating a menacing threat to his flank. He was less successful than the Romans who, a thousand years earlier, easily over-ran north Wales and immediately recognised the strategic advantages of this location. The fort established here on a four-acre site following Agricola's conquest about 78 AD, formed the southern corner of a network encompassing Snowdonia. The pivotal aspect of the fort may be appreciated by noting its radiating lines of communication: roads north-westward to Segontium (Caernarfon), northward to Caer Llugwy and Caerhun, south-eastward to Caer Gai at the SW end of Bala Lake, southward to Moridunum (Carmarthen). Tomen-y-mur was probably a training base for the entire region, as the camps at Dolddinas, 2.4km SE, would suggest — at least until about the year 120 when Roman power had been consolidated and the strategic thrust was northward — for the building of Hadrian's Wall. As part of a training complex the amphitheatre would have been used for demonstrating combat techniques.

The return trek north is worth making for its magnificent views. A full circle of ridges and summits displaying a medley of blues, greens, browns; contrasted, possibly, by a drape of mist veiling Eryri's rugged faces, with Llan and Blaenau arranged as tiny models on the landscape.

Walk 16. Rhaeadr Cynfal — Ceunant Cynfal (Cynfal Gorge) — Llan Ffestiniog. Distance : 2.1km, 1.3ml.

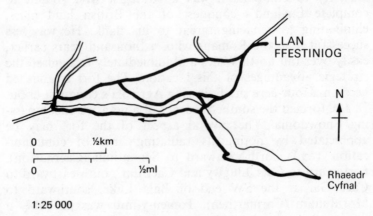

1:25 000

From the footbridge (0.0km) bear westward above the south bank along a pleasant path with stiles at 0.3km and 0.8km. Continue on 330° for 450m and turn right, down to a footbridge (1.3km) which is in deep seclusion of the ceunant, and into quietude embraced by the sound of the river.

Timelessness is here at the bottom of the gorge, a sense of what was, what is, what will be.

vii.   'Tyn ariant geunant, ar daith i'r gweunydd,
        Ei rwydi grisial o'r gwridog rosydd:
        Dirwyn ei foliant i'r cadarn foelydd,
        A'i sain bereiddia holl swyn boreddydd.

        The silver gorge draws, on a journey to meadow,
        Its crystal nets from blushing creeked moors:
        Its songs twist to indomitable hills,
        And its sound sweetens all the day's magic.

Climb up the bank E to a stile (1.4km) and then to a gate (1.5km). Veer NE to a stile (1.7km), along the edge of the field to a gate by the roadside (1.9km) and turn right to the PO.

Walk 17. Llan Ffestiniog — Ceunant Cynfal south and north. Distance : 3.7km, 2.3ml.

From Llan PO (0.0km) bear westward past the Pengwern Arms to a gate (0.2km), descend along the edge of the field (S/SW) to a stile (0.4km), SW to a gate (0.6km), descend on 240° to a stile (0.8km) and down to the footbridge. Up the south bank join the path lying E/W (0.9km), turn right (W) and enjoy the pleasant woodland with whatever thoughts that might bring.

viii. Haul gwyn ac anadl gwanwyn yn ddistaw a ddaw i ddwyn
Dyli drwy bob gwythïen, hudo o'r pridd waed i'r pren;
Annog rhuddin i'w gwreiddiau, a phuraf fêr i'w ffyrfhau,
Gwynt a haul, hwy gânt o hud siglo eu crud mwsoglyd.

White sun and breath of spring quietly will come to bring
A flux through every vein, drawing from earth blood to wood;
Enticing through roots, purest marrow to its form,
Wind and sun, incessantly rocking moss-covered cradles.

At the main road (2.0km) turn right and, beyond the bridge, right again and follow the path above the northern bank to a wall opening on the left (2.6km).

To return directly to Llan veer left through the opening and continue to the B4391 (3.2km) and along to the PO. On the bryn — or if walking E to W — a glance westward takes in the length of the Vale extending seawards between its immaculately sculptured hills clothed in native deciduous,

41

while round the half-circle northward are the summits and ridges of the Vale's head.

Alternatively, at the wall opening (2.6km) a fork right (SE) leads to another (3.3km), where the left fork trails 150m through a plantation to a gate. Bear NE to a stile (3.7km), along the edge of the field to a gate (3.9km) by the roadside (B4391) and on to the PO.

The right fork at 3.3km leads down to the footbridge at the bottom of the ceunant.

Walk 18. Llan Ffestiniog — Dduallt Railway Station. Distance : 4.7km, 3ml.

From the PO (0.0km) SW along the B4391 for 100m, turn right (NW) by the Pengwern Arms, follow the lane to its end and turn right to a gate (not the critch-cratch) on the left. Continue down the field to a gate on the right and turn left to a gate in the corner of the field (0.6km).

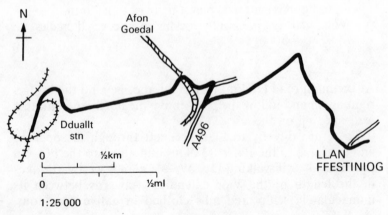

42

Bear 350° across the field to a gate (0.7km), continue to gates lower down passing a cottage on the left, NE then NW to a gate (1.0km) and turn right (N) to a barn and a path junction (1.1km)). Turn left (250°) and continue westward through a gate (1.3km) to a farm driveway (1.8km) and on to the A496. Turn sharp right and, 150m along the road, left along a driveway to a path 100m further on into the Nature Reserve, Coed Cymerau, and upstream to a footbridge (2.6km) spanning the Afon Goedal. A path winds up through woodland to a plantation submerging ruggedly textured rocks, to a stile (3.3km) and two more stiles (3.6km). Up the hill there is the bed of the old Ffestiniog line about 30m from the new route.

Standing opposite the track one may chance to hear an energetic locomotive chugging just beyond the hillside, sounding its whistle to assure the world at large that it is alive and well. Down the track 400m is Dduallt station.

The down train passes round the loop coming to rest opposite the up train which may then puff away to Tanygrisiau.

Walk 19. Dduallt station — Plas y Dduallt.
Distance : 0.7km, ½ml.

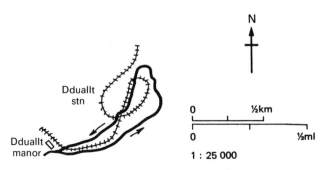

43

From the southern end of the platform (0.0km), cross the line, walk beneath the railway bridge, veer right (SW then W), enjoy a splendid view down the Vale, pass through a gate (0.5km) over the line and three stiles to arrive at Plas y Dduallt — Dduallt Manor — delightfully situated in this secluded location with a reputation of once having provided a resting place for the leader of England's revolutionary parliamentary army, Oliver Cromwell, in hot pursuit of the King's men.

Walk 20. Plas y Dduallt —
Dduallt station.
Distance : 1.6km, 1ml.

From the Manor (0.0km) walk SE and E to a gate (0.4km) and a wall (0.8km), NE and N through the woods arriving north of the loop to rejoin the route of Walk 18.

Walk 21. Dduallt station — Blaenau.
Distance : 7.7km, 4.8ml.

From the station (0.0km) follow the old railway track and the new northward to the southern end of the reservoir (1.5km), forking right round the eastern shore to a wall stile (3.3km) opposite the power station, E to a footbridge and on to the B4414 (4.1km).

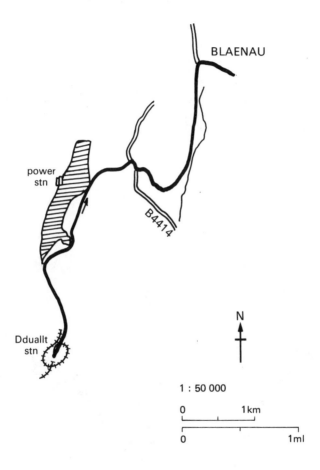

BLAENAU

power
stn

B4414

Dduallt
stn

N

1 : 50 000

0   1km

0   1ml

Turn right to a critch-cratch 200m along the road, E and
SE up and around the bryn and NE down to the valley
track. Follow the track northward along the floor of Cwm
Bowydd, up through the woods and into the town.

Walk 22.   Blaenau — Tanygrisiau
Railway Station.
Distance : 2.7km, 1.7ml.

As in Walk 1 to the B4414 and SW along the road to a stile
on the right (1.4km). Beyond the next stile veer left (250°)
and continue to a bridge over a stream which, lower down,
becomes the Afon Goedol. Turn left along the road,
continue to the PO and W past the school to the railway
station.

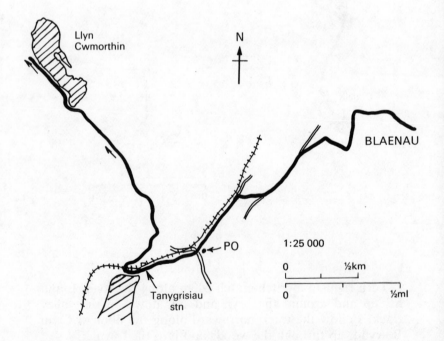

Llyn
Cwmorthin

N

BLAENAU

←PO

1:25 000

0   ½km

0   ½ml

Tanygrisiau
stn

Walk 23. Tanygrisiau — Llyn Cwmorthin and westward. Distance : 1.5km, 0.9ml.

From the railway station (0.0km) bear W to a path near the CEGB Centre, northward to a village road, turn left, then NW along the old quarry track to the southern tip of Llyn Cwmorthin (1.3km). Fork left past the ruined chapel, veer W and SW up the slope to the site of disused quarry buildings. The route westward — see **Walk in magnificent Snowdonia** — takes one past Llyn Cwmcorsiog and on to the enchanting Llyn yr Adar — lake of birds — elevation 2000ft, and down into the Nantgwynant Valley and Beddgelert (13.5km 8½ml) through fields of wild rhododendrons.

Tanygrisiau

Grisiau, meaning stairs, refers to the gradients of all routes westward. *Tanygrisiau* : under the stairs, which you together with your packhorse, must climb step by step.

In the early nineteenth century a village was born as rows of houses clinging to rocks near the site of a quarry. Now, Tanygrisiau has a new purpose as a base for the Central Electricity Generating Board's hydro-electric power operation. The system uses two lakes, one higher, the other lower. Power is generated as water from the top lake, Llyn Stwlan, drains to the artificially created Tanygrisiau reservoir. During off-peak periods at night, excess power from the national grid is used to pump water back to Stwlan for further generation.

In playing its new role, Tanygrisiau retains the feel of its traditional character : steep grades, terraces, the shop and post office, the railway station and the steam train with its re-assuring whistle. One could not mistake this place for somewhere else. Tanygrisiau is unique.

Walk 24. Tanygrisiau round the reservoir. Distance : 5.3km, 3.3ml.

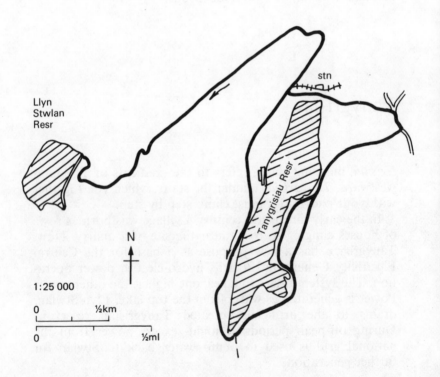

From the station (0.0km) turn right past the CEGB Centre, fork left (0.2km), veer left at 0.7km to a footbridge and stile (0.8km) and on to stiles on either side of the railway line (0.9km) opposite the power station. Continue southward past the occasional angler in pursuit of rainbow trout to a footbridge at the southern end (2.1km).

Returning round the eastern side brings one to a fork (2.9km) : westward round the shore, or north-eastward? Both routes converge at a stepped wall stile (3.8km, taking the shore route). Continue E to a footbridge, on to the B4414 (4.6km) and turn left to the railway station.

Walk 25. Tanygrisiau — Llyn Stwlan weir.
Distance : 3km, 1.9ml.

Allow the environment to induce reflection. Gushing waterfalls draping massive boulders in silky, wispy white. From all directions, rugged ridges commanding attention. Capricious mists lying off awaiting a propitious moment to descend.

The eyes keep returning from distant horizons to this Moelwyn massif, to mighty molars meticulously placed in monumental stone walls carrying tracks along which wealth was extracted from this place. The massive manual input expended in times before machinery makes the mind boggle. Such labour!

One feels that those nameless labourers with no memorials should not be forgotten; unsaluted; unsung.

Now, the only work done on the cliff faces is that of rock climbers practising their skills.

Walk along the top of the weir, down and around.

Where are the birds? Why do they shun this place? A mouthful of water from a gurgling stream feeding the reservoir leaves a dry peaty taste. One searches around the rocks as on a seashore when the tide is out. Where are the creatures burrowing, skurrying, freezing into immobility in defence? Rising water during the time of surplus power provides no haven for there is no life here.

One watches the mist descending, doing its best to shroud the CEGB installation, trying to claim its own.

Walk 26. Tanygrisiau — Dduallt.
Distance : 4.4km, 2¾ml.

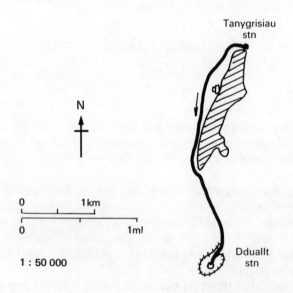

Continue as for Walk 24 to the southern end of the reservoir (2.1km). Follow the track E then S to a gate and stile (2.5km), then soar above the level of the railway and plunge

50

lower than it as an immaculately crafted stone causeway appears on the left. This was the route of the old Ffestiniog line before the construction of Tanygrisiau reservoir. We have the privilege of joining it (3.1km), stepping over the old sleepers still in place. Then appears the Dduallt station (3.6km) and that incredible phenomenon which will bear renewed contemplation — the Dduallt loop.

In the old days before the introduction of steam power this would have enabled two narrow-gauge trains to pass so that an unpowered down train kept gravitational momentum. What a fantastic device! Stand at the centre of the loop, where a direction dial has been erected on the mound reserved for viewing and picnicking, and see how magnificently it works.

From the southern end of the platform (3.7km) continue to Plas y Dduallt as in Walk 19.

Walk 27.   Plas y Dduallt to the valley road.
Distance : 1km, 5 furlongs.

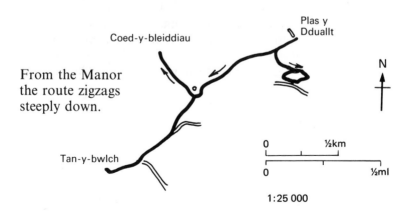

From the Manor the route zigzags steeply down.

Coed-y-bleiddiau

Plas y Dduallt

Tan-y-bwlch

N

0   ½km

0   ½ml

1:25 000

51

Walk 28.   Plas y Dduallt — Tan-y-bwlch.
Distance : 2km, 1¼ml.

From the Manor (0.0km) along the drive (250°) to a stile (0.4km), down to a footbridge spanning a silky stream issuing from a sparkling waterfall on the right. Continue W through the delightful Coedydd Maentwrog to a gate, turn right (W) past the cottage Bwthyn Bronturnor and over a footbridge (1.1km), fork left (SW) to a gate by the valley road and on to Tan-y-bwlch.

Walk 29.   Plas y Dduallt — Coed-y-bleiddiau.
Distance : 1.6km, 1ml.

As in Walk 28 to the footbridge (1.1km), fork right (W) up the hill, up and around a rocky outcrop, across the upper contours of a deep valley and NW to join the route of Walk 30 in *Coed-y-bleiddiau* — the wood of wolves, a name for this part of the forest that must be as old as Maentwrog across the valley.

In the churchyard are three large yew trees reputably more than 1000 years old. They shelter the graves of the Oakleys, creators of the village we see today.

William Griffith Oakley (1790-1835), son of a quarry master, was an aesthete who sought harmony between human construction and the environment. He personally supervised extraction of long blocks of stone, the shaping and dressing, then the careful fitting into walls with a minimum use of mortar. The Oakleys were fortunate in their choice of site — and so are we — for the high ground to the south and east, and low river plain to the north and west, preclude the type of twentieth-century development that would spoil this village.

The Oakley's home was at Plas Tan-y-bwlch, successor of earlier houses that represented the centre of an estate extending over a wide area of Eryri from Llanfrothen to Dolwyddelan. In the sixteenth century the incumbent squire was a descendant of the Welsh Prince Gruffydd ap Cynan, defender of Gwynedd against the intruder, King William II. It was a meeting place for bards where literary talents were fostered and generous hospitality provided. Then, in the eighteenth century a daughter married William Oakley from Staffordshire and a new era began : into quarrying, land improvement and architecture. It was a fortunate development in that although the new arrivals were not mere seekers after wealth, upon acquiring it they had the talent to use it well. They sought to practise artistic excellence in their surroundings.

Walk 30. Plas y Dduallt — Tan-y-bwlch Railway Station.
Distance : 3.2km, 2ml.

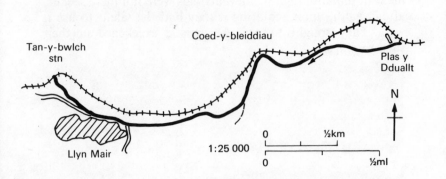

Tan-y-bwlch stn

Coed-y-bleiddiau

Plas y Dduallt

Llyn Mair

N

1:25 000

0   ½km

0   ½ml

Fork right from the Manor (0.0km) to a stile (0.1km), on to a stream (0.3km) and into the Nature Reserve. The trail lies along an upper edge of the Vale close to the Ffestiniog railway line whose passengers are borne past fleetingly, leaving one to enjoy the expanse.

Beyond Coed y Bleiddiau cottage (1.0km), veer SW from the line, take a right fork (1.3km) and endure a transition from hardwood broadleaf to spruce pine.

Continue down to the B4410 (2.4km) and along the northern shore of beautiful Llyn Mair, named, so legend relates, because an unfortunate girl, Mair, submerged herself in response to unrequited love. Veer right (2.7km) into the centuries-old woodland known as Coed Llyn Mair. Cross the footbridge (3.0km) that spans a stream of pure crystal and continue to Tan-y-bwlch station.

TAN-Y-BWLCH   confluence of
                    ANCIENT
                    PRESENT
                    FUTURE

Breathe the clean air — despite the railway and its steam locomotives and a main road lying alongside the shore of the lake — and note that on the bark of some trees are grey patches of lichens — evidence that the air really is unpolluted.

Looking southward from the station the woodland represents a fragment of how parts of high-rainfall Britain appeared after the Ice Age and before the age of industrialism.

Oak, the greatest British host for bird and insect life, has reproduced on this patch of ground, together with other natural hardwoods, for hundreds of years providing examples for study of nature in pure form.

Walk 31. Tan-y-bwlch Railway Station — via Coedydd Maentwrog to east Penrhyndeudraeth. Distance : 4.3km, 2.7ml.

From the station (0.0km) walk SE along the path of the nature trail, established by the Nature Conservancy Council, leading to a stile (0.1km) and a footbridge by the B4410 (0.4km). Turn right (NW), past the turnoff to Tan-y-bwlch station (0.8km), under the railway bridge (0.9km) advertising its 1854 origin in the Boston Lodge Foundry, past the turnoff to Croesor and Beddgelert (1.0km). Five hundred metres along the road turn left (S) onto plantation land where, because of fire, members of marching pine battalions

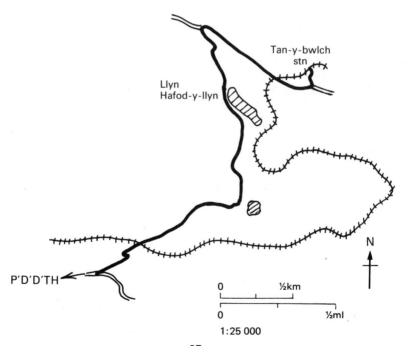

stand dead (in 1985) enabling native plants to reclaim their own territory. Under the charred bodies of invaders, sapling growths of oak, birch, rowan, blackberry are flourishing.

Approaching a wall opening (1.9km) veer left (SE) with the wall on the right. Above Llyn Hafod-y-llyn veer to SW and hope to find a path if it has not been destroyed by planters. At a wall opening and stile (2.1km) take the fork SE and turn sharp right (W) then S and continue with pleasant hardwood and rhododendron on the right and encroaching pine on the left. There is an attractive view down to the SE end of the lake and a strangely incongruous sound of a steam locomotive puffing away a little more than a hundred yards somewhere beyond the wall of trees. One may divert down to the railway at 2.5km. A feature of this route is that, like the railway, it follows the contours.

There is a path-crossing at 2.8km, and 400m further on one meets a forestry road which has obliterated part of the path. Turn right (NW) along the road for 100m; turn left (S), by-passing a small lake on the left (3.3km). Continue on 250° for 300m, veer left from the wide path (still on 250°) down through the woods to a wall opening and, beyond it, stiles on either side of the railway line (3.7km). Continue down a steep path, including a zigzag, through the woods to a gate (4.2km) and the A487. Penrhyndeudraeth lies a little more than a mile south-westward.

PENRHYNDEUDRAETH   *COCKLES*
                INDEPENDENCE
        RADICAL TRADITION

On that neck of land which at one time was almost surrounded by sea — *penrhyn* means promontory or cape — there was a community known as "*cocosiaid y Penrhyn*" — the cockles of Penrhyn. They were gatherers of cockles from the extensive stretches of beach sands to the north and south. To the north is *Traeth Mawr* — big beach, to the south *Traeth Bach* — small beach. *Penrhyndeudraeth:* cape between two beaches.

The two beaches were referred to in a book by Gerallt Gymro who travelled through Wales with Archbishop Baldwin in 1198.

Penrhyndeudraeth was identified under that name on a list of rates imposed by the conquering English king, Edward the First, in 1291.

Over the centuries, these isolated folk lived on their cape with two imperatives : subjection to the landlord and survival through self-sufficiency by working their plots and gathering a harvest from the sea. It was a background that — apparently — nurtured independent minds and a radical tradition.

A wind of change arrived in the eighteenth century with the ever-rising demand for slate, followed early in the following century by the building of the cob across the estuary. Linkage with the outside world brought change and opportunity. Penrhyndeudraeth developed downwards from the high ground, known as Cefn Coch, to the flat land below which had been drained by a local landowner — David Williams, Castelldeudraeth — later to become the local Member of Parliament.

Williams, although hardly a radical, was regarded by Penrhyn people as representative of their interests against those of absentee landlords who bribed, intimidated and punished in order to retain their hold on the parliamentary seat. Following the 1867 Reform Act, and consequent extension of the franchise, Williams of Penrhyndeudraeth was sent to parliament in the election of 1868.

Today, this community's roots show up like an irrepressible stream in its responses to the movements of our times. What is of concern to the country and the world is not ignored here behind the estuary of the two rivers. And the bards continue singing.

ix.   Y ffin a welaf tros aber dwy afon
        O benrhyn Llyn hyd ein traethell heno'n
        Llwybr awennau lle bu Rhiannon
        A'i hadar can hyd-ddo'n trydar cwynion
        Alaeth yr hen gwerylon; — ffin liw rhudd,
        A lliw'r hwyrddydd yw lloriau Iwerddon.

        The boundary I see over the estuary of two rivers
        From Llyn peninsula to our beach tonight
        The path of lore trodden by Rhiannon
        Along with her song birds chirping laments
        Sorrows of old quarrels; — a crimson boundary
        And the colour of eventide on the floors of Ireland.

Walk 32.   Penrhyndeudraeth — Rhyd.
Distance : 3km, 1.9ml.

From the Penrhyn Railway Station (0.0km), cross the road
E, descend steps, turn left (N/NE). At 0.4km veer right, up
steps and continue N under the railway line (0.5km). Turn
right (N), right again (E), fork right, veer left (0.6km),
continue on 060° to a gate (0.9km), a farmhouse (1.5km) and
a gate (1.6km).

Alternatively, this walk may be commenced from a point
one mile NE from Penrhyndeudraeth on the A487 (GR
626401). A cart track bears 010° to the Ffestiniog Railway
line (0.5km). Cross the line to the track bearing 060° from
the village.

Walking this path one may hear a sharp bang and see a puff of smoke rise from behind a ridge to the south. This would be *bone fide* explosive makers testing their product. The explosive works was established last century in response to a growing demand from the quarries and has been in production ever since — a singular example of industrial continuity.

From the plantation boundary gate (2.0km), through gates at 2.5km and 2.7km one discovers the pleasant hamlet of Rhyd.

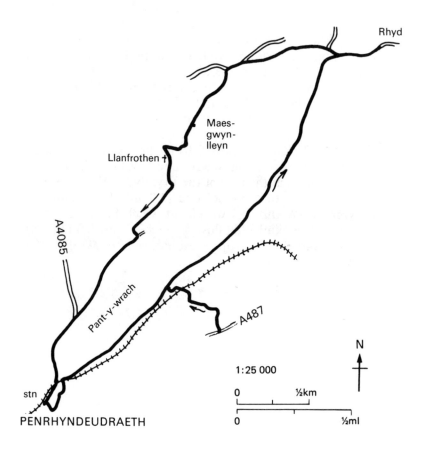

Walk 33.   Rhyd — Llanfrothen — Penrhyndeudraeth.
Distance : 4.5km, 2.9ml.

From Rhyd (0.0km) walk W to a stile (0.4km) at the side of the road and on the same bearing over three more stiles to a gate at the roadside (1.1km), turn left and, 100m along, left again (190°), veer to 240° and continue beside the right bank of the stream over a stile (1.5km) to another by the cottage Maes Gwyr Lleyn (1.7km). Continue down the drive to a gate (1.9km) and turn right to Llanfrothen. Should this village appear abandoned, giving an impression of ghosts in the churchyard, it might be as well to know that it is the centre of a wide area extending northward to Croesor and southward to Penrhyndeudraeth. Within that area there are cottage industries, not to mention a hotel soon to be discovered.

Turn left (2.1km) and bear S from the rear of the church over a footbridge, veering to 210° and SW. At 2.7km join a track originating at the rear of the Brynllydan Hotel, veer to SE and continue to a public road (3.0km). Turn right (S), then veer to SW through woodland which bears the name *Pant-y-wrach* (3.5km) — hollow of witches. Veer left (3.8km) along the A4058 across the Ffestiniog line (4.3km) to the Penrhyn station.

Walk 34.   Penrhyn Station — Ty-obry
— Bwlch-glas — Penrhyn.
Distance : 6.3km, 4ml.

From Penrhyn station (0.0km) cross the line, turn right
(NE), veer left then right (0.2km), continue northward to a
gate (0.3km) and a wall stile (0.4km). Further north 100m
the path joins another beginning 100m east at the side of the
B3310.

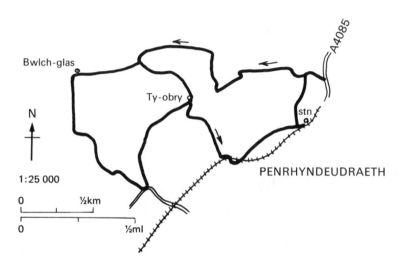

Continue W to a fence corner (0.6km), veer right through
a gate to a farm drive, *Cae Merched* (0.8km) — field of
women, W up the field to a stile (0.9km) and along the
mound behind the farmhouse (1.0km). Veer to SW and
continue through woodland to a plantation boundary stile
(1.3km). This leads through the plantation to a farmhouse,
Ty-obry, a distance of 300m. *Ty-obry* : the house below.
Nearby is *Ty-fry* : the house above.

Alternatively from 1.3km, turn right along the outside of the plantation boundary to a stile (1.4km), northward down to a gate (1.7km), turn left (NW to W) and at 2.2km turn left again and follow a road winding south-eastward to Ty-obry (2.9km).

Alternatively at 2.2km, turn left then right over a cattle grid, passing the house Bwlch-glas (2.7km) on the right, turn left over a stile (2.8km) and continue S across the cob to a gate (3.2km) at the edge of the woods. Turn left (E) and continue S then SE through the woods to a road (3.9km). Turn left and left again (northward) past a caravan park on the left to a fork right (4.7km) onto a grass path and sharp right by the farmhouse, Ty-obry, up a broad grass slope bearing SW then S to a gate (5.0km), SE and S to a plantation boundary gate (5.3km).

Continue southward then E under the railway bridge (5.6km), turn left (NE) at 5.7km to a stile and veer right (E) alongside the railway, through a chapel's grounds and left to the Penrhyn station.

Walk 35. The estuary.
Distance : 2.2km, 1.4ml.

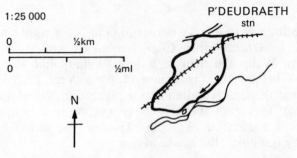

1:25 000

0   ½km

0   ½ml

N

From Penrhyndeudraeth's British Rail mainline station (0.0km), walk W for 100m, turn left (SW) across the railway line, SW past the house *Craig-y-don* — Rock of the wave, veer right (0.8km) then left to a critch-cratch (0.9km) and W across the flat of the estuary to a stile (1.2km) at the edge of the woods.

Turn right across the Cambrian railway line to a stile (1.3km), continue NE to a critch-cratch and on to the mainline station.

Walk 36. Minffordd — Portmeirion — Boston Lodge.
Distance : 3km, 1.9ml.

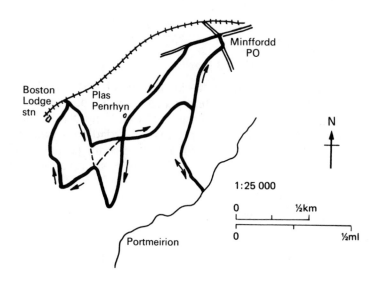

From Minffordd PO (0.0km), walk 300m W along the A497, turn left (SW) into a lane and fork left at 0.8km to Plas Penrhyn (0.9km).

This Regency house was acquired by Bertrand Russell in 1955 and it was from here that Russell, in the late nineteen-fifties and early 'sixties, sent off messages to world heads of state concerning the preservation of international peace. It is thought that one of the reasons Russell was attracted to the area, and to Plas Penrhyn, was its association with the poet Shelley, who lived across the estuary at Tan-yr-allt above Tremadog — in 1812/13.

Continue 200m to the stables where paths diverge, and S to the boundary of the Portmeirion park (1.5km). Veer NW and W then SW (1.8km), and enjoy fine views of the estuary to Boston Lodge Railway Station.

Walk 37.   Boston Lodge — Minffordd.
Distance : 2km, 1¾ml.

From the railway station (0.0km), veer left (SE) at 0.1km and continue 300m to a gate, turn left (E) to a path junction at the stables (0.7km), on to a gate (1.0km) and NE through the woods to a road (1.3km). Cross the road to a junction (1.4km). (The path southward past Cae-canol (200m), and then SE, is an attractive walk to the estuary shore, a distance of 700m)

Turn left from the junction (1.4km) and continue north-eastward to Minffordd.

CRICIETH   *SENSE*
              A HEROIC
              AGE

This village is not in the Vale of Ffestiniog so why come here
to begin an exploration of the Vale's seaward end? There are
three reasons.

One is that on the top of the knoll behind which Cricieth shelters from the sea is a significant monument : the remains of a Welsh castle constructed by Wales's greatest leader, Llywelyn Fawr, in the early thirteenth century and later extended by the English following their conquest. Although a ruin it is an important relic of Wales's heroic age.

Another is that the farthest seaward expression of the Vale, Graig Ddu Traeth — Black Rock Sands, that magnificent expanse of beach which many people enjoy in summer, may be approached on foot from Cricieth via Graig Ddu itself and discovered in the manner of a revelation.

The third reason for coming to Cricieth is Moel Ednyfed, a hill behind the village which provides an opportunity to observe contrasts and proportions over a wide expanse of the area.

Walk 38.   Cricieth Castle —
Moel Ednyfed.
Distance : 2.2km, 1.4ml.

From the castle entrance (0.0km) bear N across the A497 along the B4411 to a turning right (1.2km) into a lane leading NE to Cefniwrch and a gate (1.3km), and on through several critch-cratches : along the edge of the field and a choice of routes to the summit.

The view seawards takes in most of Cardigan Bay, including the linear expanse of Black Rock and Harlech Sands, while the remainder of the full circle is a panorama of summits and ridges. In the immediate foreground Cricieth nestles like a faithful support platoon behind its castle.

Descend from the summit bearing 160° to a critch-cratch in the corner of the field, E along the field boundary to a gate and turn right (S) to Cricieth.

Walk 39. Cricieth Castle — Graig Ddu — Black Rock Sands.
Distance : 3km, 1.9ml.

From the castle entrance (0.0km) walk E to the end of the esplanade (0.8km), and the gate by the railway crossing (0.9km), eastward along the path and across the line at 1.5km. At 1.8km there is a diversion NE which leads to the A497 via the farm Ystumllyn, offering a silhouette view of Moel-y-gest and its summit massif which awaits our ascent.

Continuing south-eastward, cross the line and bear 160° round the seaward side of Graig Ddu and up to the cliff top above the cave.

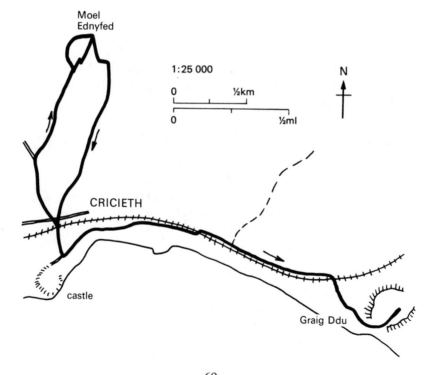

Graig Ddu and Black Rock Sands offer wonderful
locations for contemplation of shore, sea and sky. Especially
in calm conditions at the approach of evening when summer
has departed.

x.   Tu allan, gwylan yn hwylio o'r golwg
heibio i'r Trwyn : neb ar y traeth :
yr hir ewyn yn derwyn wrth dorri :
y lliwiau yn nef y gorllewin —
aur mâl, tân a phorffor a melyn
a rhos yr hwyrnos — yn rhyw
bylu'n araf fel y suddai'r belen eirias
tu ôl i gaerau tawel y gorwel,
caerau o gymylau a'u myrdd
o dyrau yn dyrau o dan :
petrus sêr : ym mhellter y môr
hwyl wen ar fin diflannu
o'r hwyrnos a'r rhuddwawr arni.

Outside, a seagull sailing out of sight
beyond the cape : no-one on the beach :
the long foam brilliant when breaking :
the colours in the western sky —
wrought gold, fire and purple and yellow
and the rose of evening — somehow
dimming slowly as the molten ball sinks
behind quiet citadels of the horizon,
forts of clouds and their myriads
of towers being towers of fire :
uncertain stars : in distant sea
a white sail on brink of disappearing
from the evening taking its red hue.

In Porthmadog, amidst bustle in Stryd Fawr, one feels a need of height and space to consider this historic port in relation to the broad sweep of its surroundings. So, let the thrust be outward until a point is reached where one may take stock and contemplate.

Walk 40. Porthmadog — Tremadog.
Distance : 3km, 1.9ml.

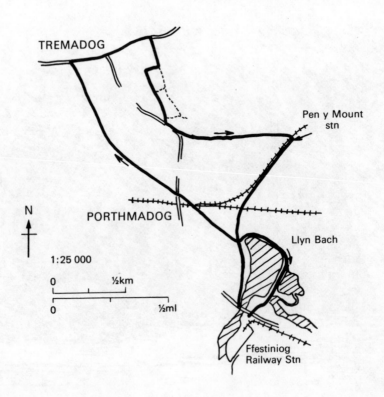

From the town side of the bridge that spans the Afon Glaslyn (0.0km), walk northward. At 0.6km there is a fork right (N/NE) which is on the return route if Walk 41 is followed. From the next junction (0.8km) the path lies alongside Y Cyt — The Cut — which was designed to form a convenient transport link between two communities in the days when a canal was the most up-to-date transport mode. Now, alas, this canal is much overgrown.

There is a stile (1.1km) adjacent to the British Rail Cambrian line and the Welsh Highland Light Railway Station, both lines meeting at this point. Cross the road (A487), fork right (340°) at 1.9km, continue to the main road (2.6km) and turn right to Tremadog.

TREMADOG   *IMAGINATION   PERCEPTION*
                        RESOLUTION

The name is said to derive from Madog ap Owain Gwynedd who, according to tradition, sailed to the coast of America in the twelfth century. By coincidence, the name suggests the town's founder, William Alexander Madocks (1773-1828), Member of Parliament for Boston, Lincolnshire.

The concept of the Vale, as seen in human construction and operation today, is essentially that of Madocks more than any other individual. Madocks designed Tremadog. In the early nineteenth century he built the Cyt connecting Tremadog with what was to become the thriving port of Porthmadog. In 1807, he secured authority via a special Act of Parliament to build an embankment, now known as the Cob, across the estuary. About 5,000 acres of land were thereby reclaimed from the sea and a route was provided for the transport of slate by railway from the Ffestiniog quarries to the coast. This necessitated the building of port facilities and Porthmadog became part of a worldwide trading network.

However, Madocks' essential characteristic was that, like the Oakleys of Maentwrog, he sought to harmonise human construction with the environment. Look at Tremadog's spacious town square and well-designed buildings. The constructive imagination of the man inspired Percy Shelley who had taken the house, Tan-yr-allt, where he started to write his famous work Queen Mab. Shelley felt inspired by Madocks' philosophy and set about raising funds from local landowners in support of the embankment project. He also contributed from his own money despite personal indebtedness. Such was the poet's romantic idealism.

But still one must seek for a height in order to appreciate Madocks' grand concept.

Walk 41.   Tremadog — Pen y Mount — Porthmadog.
Distance : 4.7km, 3ml.

From Tremadog Square (0.0km) walk E for 400m and turn right (S) to a fork (0.6km). Southwards there are paths circulating these attractive woods. Fork right (W), then left (S) at 0.7km to the main road (1.2km), turn left, left again 100m further on and fork right (E). This lane leads to the present terminus, Pen y Mount (2.4km), of the Welsh Highland Light Railway which once connected Porthmadog to Beddgelert and Caernarfon, and is now in process of restoration.

From Pen y Mount station continue SW to the stile by the railway workshop (2.8km) — Gelert's Farm Works — and on to join the route of Walk 40 near the northern end of the tidal pool known as *Llyn Bach* — small lake. Turn left then fork right 100m further on, round the eastern side of Llyn Bach from where there is a good view of the old town and its protective mountain, Moel-y-gest, behind it. Cross the footbridge above the tidal sluice gates, where power is not generated from the twice daily inward and outward flow, to the Ffestiniog Railway Station.

THE WONDER KEEPS ROLLING

The cheerfulness is infectious. Whether it is a guard's greeting as the train pulls into Tanygrisiau, a driver's wave from a locomotive in Coedydd Maentwrog, a sales assistant's smile at Tan-y-bwlch, or the pages of the quarterly magazine : the overwhelming impression is that these folk are enjoying themselves! What, one asks oneself, is the source of such feelings of well-being?

The amazing triumph of idealism following the official closure of the railway in 1946 is a story well told elsewhere. Technical feats there were a-plenty. What remains in human terms is enduring enthusiasm and, to an observer wanting to understand why this has happened, a feeling that there is something just beyond the mind's grasp. Of course there is a wellspring of joy flowing from successful co-operative achievement. But that could not explain the continuing devotion which this society enjoys.

Could it be that at the centre of the operation is participation? Anyone can join in, become a volunteer, take part in a successful process, learn how to do things, enjoy collective effort, see practical results. The harmonious working together of paid staff with volunteers leaves one wondering if this is not an achievement as significant as the restoration itself.

This oldest passenger-carrying, narrow-gauge railway in the world is justly world famous : a wonderful example of resilience. But one continues to feel that the phenomenon is not wholly explainable, that somewhere, tucked away in the human spirit is a nucleus as fathomable, or unfathomable, as that other nucleus, and with comparable potential too.

Walk 42. Porthmadog — Moel-y-gest summit.
Distance : 7.5km, 4.7ml.

Leave Stryd Fawr — Porthmadog High Street — near Y Ganolfan (0.0km) and walk along and around dockland. But alas:

xi.　　　　　Aur hwyl ni throedia'r heli :
　　　　　　Ni ddaw llong dros ymchwydd lli,
　　　　　　Na llawen nwyf y rhwyfwr
　　　　　　Dewr ei daith hyd war y dŵr.

　　　　　　No gold sail graces the sea :
　　　　　　No ship rides the swelling tide,
　　　　　　Neither is there an oarsman
　　　　　　Setting out on the water.

It is a yacht basin now and beyond the haven is an array of mainly marine-associated industries and workshops, a busy place on a weekday morning. This labour-intensive scene suddenly gives way to sedate residential suburbia of discreetly spaced houses. When a pleasant bay appears — if the tide is in — we discover that we have entered the seaside resort of Borth-y-gest (1.3km). Nothing discordant here; just an impression of pleasantness, sobriety, serenity.

On the farther side of the bay we pass the church (1.8km) onto a seafront path, forking right (2.1km) and, 100m further on, right (NW) to meet a broad path (2.4km).

Westward, the path continues amongst sand dune and seascape. But our destination is a mountain summit and, therefore, we must negotiate a spread of caravan parks. By a park corner veer right (N/NE), reaching a critch-cratch and the road (3.4km) near *Llyn Gareg Wen* — lake of the white stone. Here, we have a choice of route.

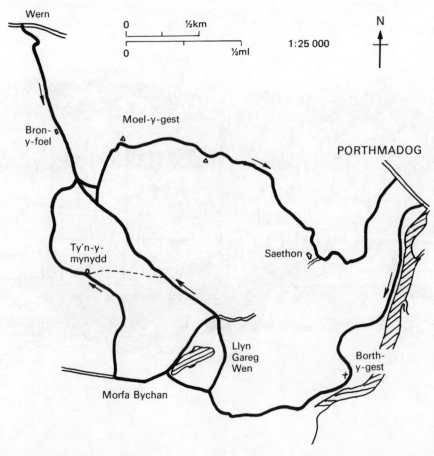

Turning left, continue for about 800m, turn right and face the summit dead ahead north.

Alternatively from the park corner, continue to the SW tip of Llyn Gareg Wen, which appears wedged into the road fork, turn left and, about 300m along, turn right as above.

Fork left at 5.2m, veer right at 5.3km and right again at 5.5km. We now wind along and across the contours, ever upward.

One thing about this mountain is its truthfulness. It presents challengers with its true summit, honestly facing them in full frontal candour; not like some sly moels which proffer false summits while keeping the real one back.

And this moel is generous too. After passing the highest farm cottage, *Ty'n-y-mynydd* (6.1km) — house on the mountain — it offers its garden. If one is walking in the season of bloom, every colour of heather will be presented on this south-facing aspect: deep red, maroon, browns, fawns, purples, white.

xii.   Tlws eu tw', liaws tawel, — gemau teg
          Gwmwd haul ac awel,
          Crog glychau'r creigle uchel,
          Fflur y main, ffiolau'r mêl.

      Beautiful, quiet multitude, — fine gems
          Domain of sun and breeze,
          Hanging bells of the high rock,
          Slender flowers, phials of honey.

Beyond a stile (6.7km), there is a gate 100m further on at the base of the summit massif.

Alternatively at the Morfa Bychan road (3.4km), cross to a wall stile and bear NW on a broad path to a gate (4.8km) beyond which the path forks. The left fork leads, in 700m, to the farm cottage Ty'n-y-mynydd and joins with the path described above about 100m beyond the cottage to the NW. The right fork leads NW to a gate (5.3km) and a wall stile (5.6km) where one turns right (N) to the gate at the base of the summit massif.

This small mountain has yet another gift to bestow: an interesting and easy rock climb up its summit massif to the top.

Walk 43. Wern — Moel-y-gest Summit.
Distance : 2km, 1 ¼ml.

From a point on the A497 near Wern (0.0km) walk up the farm track, forking left at 0.9km onto a green path rising from the farmhouse Bron-y-foel, then to a gate (1.4km), a wall opening (1.5km), E to the gate where these routes converge and up the rocks to the summit.

From the Moel-y-gest summit *Mynydd Ednyfed* behind Cricieth is a mere pimple on the landscape. *Morfa Bychan* is a flat square sandwich on the immense sweep of Cardigan Bay. *Borth-y-gest* is the tiny fishing village it once was. This is a place to review one's sense of proportion. Opportunities for doing so are unusual because Moel-y-gest has two summits, western and eastern, with a connecting ridge which provides excellent viewing.

Walk 44. Moel-y-gest West Summit — East Summit.
Distance : 1.2km, ¾ml.

Moving east from the west summit (0.0km) one realises that this moel is just the right size for its locality, not being so high that it overpowers its surroundings while providing suitable distance for detached intimacy. Down there at the foot of Craig y Castell, below the house, Tan-yr-allt, where Shelley lived, is William Madocks' Tremadog. Madocks was one of those few individuals whose work endures. He planned Tremadog as a model community and from this height one can see a broad square and wide streets with the Cyt forming a logical transport link to the seaboard, and, ultimately, to the world. Fortunately, the modern development southwards blends with Madocks' design — almost as if the planner had himself foreseen the kind of challenges with which his creation would have to contend.

One can imagine a single mind working to an overall concept of two communities, linked but playing separate roles, set harmoniously in a broad expanse of hinterland. It was a response to a basic commercial stimulus that is now past.

A bard sings of what is everlasting.

xiii.   Mae'r llanw'n dal i ddyfod,
               A chilio'n ol yn slei,
          Gan adael sawrau gwymon
               I loetran lond y cei;
          A chyffry'r cychod bach am dro
          O'u gogwydd diog ar y gro.

          The tide rises as ever,
               And withdraws slyly,
          Leaving odours of seaweed
               Loitering over the quay;
          And rousing small boats to life
          From slumbers on the gravel.

He laments for the past.

Ac nid oes neb yn tremio'n
    Ddisgwylgar dros y bar,
Fe ddarfu'r son am 'Frisco,
    Brisbane a Zanzibar;
'Does neb yn malio mwy am sgorn
Y moryn hwnnw gylch yr Horn.

And there is no-one gazing
    Watchfully over the bar,
Vanished the talk of 'Frisco,
    Brisbane and Zanzibar;
No-one feels moved by the scorn
Of that sea about the Horn.

He sings joyously for the present.

Mae rheiliau'r Cob yn tasgu
    Dan dywyn haul y nawn,
A Prins yn tynnu'n galed
    A'r holl gerbydau'n llawn;
Mae'r hen dren bach yn talu'n dda
A'i siwrnai'n 'mestyn Ha' 'rol Ha'.

The rails of the Cob shimmer
    Beneath the afternoon sun,
And Prince is pulling strongly
    With all his carriages full;
The *tren bach* is paying well
Its line advancing each year.

Now the line has reached its terminus at the head of the Vale, bringing a new significance to this old port.

One has to remind oneself that that oblong patch of buildings has three railways which, surely, must be an imcomparable distinction. The smallest, with stout heart and mighty ambition, is apt to make the most noise, possibly because its engine is continually changing ends to serve its very short stretch of line from Porthmadog to Pen y Mount, a distance of barely a mile. But the future stretches away into the distance along the route northward across Traeth Mawr and on to Beddgelert which was settled way back in the mists of time, more than a thousand years ago, by monks looking for peace and quiet. While cherishing tranquillity and seclusion from the secular world they created a priory which endured for many centuries but had disappeared long before the highland railway arrived on the scene.

Walk 45. East Summit of Moel-y-gest
        — Porthmadog.
        Distance : 4km, 2½ml.

Reluctantly, one takes leave of this place, descending into a garden of heathers, if here in the season of bloom; tacking across a scree of boulders, down to a path (1.9km), then to a wall stile (2.0km), a fence stile (2.3km), past Saethon (3.0km) to Stryd Fawr.

Walk 46. Porthmadog — Beddgelert.
Distance : 15km, 9.4ml.

From the Welsh Highland Railway Station (0.0km) walk SE for 300m, turn left (NE) over the bridge, cross the British Rail line (0.5km), continue past Gelert's Farm Works of the W.H.L.R. on the left and follow the path to Pen y Mount Station.

Following the course of the old railway along its embankment one passes over stiles every two to three hundred metres to a stile at 2.9km. Veer left to the next stile (3.1km), then to a critch-cratch (3.2km) near the course of a winding stream, turn right to a gate and left along the railway embankment. Beyond a stile at 3.8km one arrives at the Afon Glaslyn (4.5km) — Pont Croesor, an objective of restoration for the railway company in its long haul up the valley. Here a broad river will have to be bridged, a river which, when it overflows its banks flooding adjacent flat fields, creates an impression of how this area must have appeared when Traeth Mawr was under the sea.

Along a stretch of road adjacent to the old railway track is a stile at 5.7km from which continue, veering from 070° to 040°.

At 7.2km veer left to 310°, and at 7.7km there is a long curve to 340°, leading to an undecked bridge (8.0km), and, 200m further on, one crosses the bridge spanning the Afon Dylif, a tributary of the Glaslyn. The next bridge (8.9km), across the Afon Nanmor, another tributary of the Glaslyn, has been decked and gated as a footbridge. The track veers round hillocks (N) to a stile (9.2km), then, on 340°, round wooded low cliffs to 025° and a straight stretch until we arrive near to the Afon Glaslyn (10.8km) where there is a stile; then along an embankment to an undecked bridge across the A4085 (11.3km). Continue through a cutting, over an embankment on a short curve to 325°, through another cutting to 345° and a straight stretch crossing the Nantmor Road (11.9km); then through cuttings, across a high

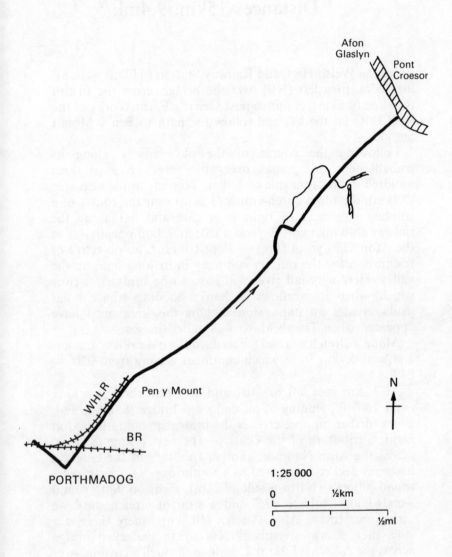

Afon
Glaslyn

Pont
Croesor

N

Pen y Mount

WHLR

BR

PORTHMADOG

1:25 000

0   ½km

0   ½ml

86

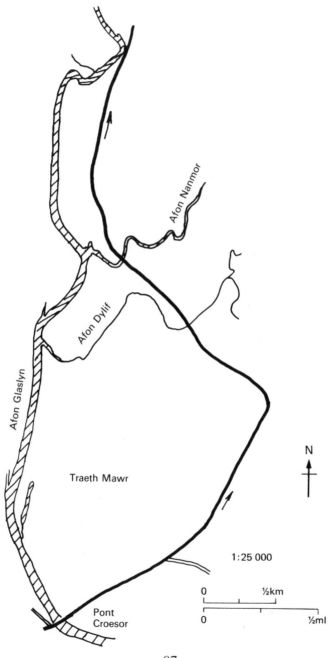

Afon Nanmor

Afon Dylif

Afon Glaslyn

Traeth Mawr

N

1:25 000

0   ½km

0   ½ml

Pont
Croesor

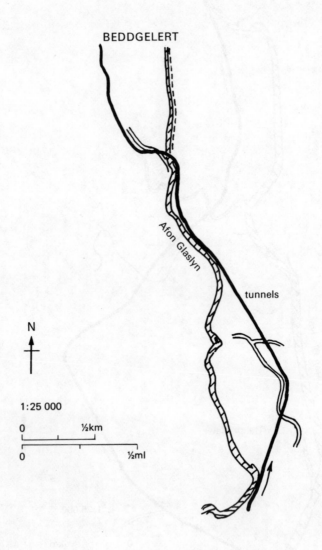

BEDDGELERT

Afon Glaslyn

tunnels

N

1:25 000

0   ½km

0   ½ml

embankment and into a tunnel (12.2km) with no light at the end of it.

Proceeding hopefully, the way ahead lightens round the tunnel bend. After emerging (12.6km) one enters two short stretches of tunnel and then, if we happen to be here in May or early June, a display of wild rhododendron on the west-facing hillsides can be enjoyed. Copper is thought to be the nutrient that causes the brilliant blooming. The mineral was mined here by a German company before the First World War and some of the shafts, of what were then known as the Sygun copper mines, can still be seen.

Now it is time to cross the Glaslyn via another railway bridge (13.7km), continue under a road bridge carrying the A498, through a long-curved cutting and along the base of the hillsides to our destination near the rear of the Royal Goat Hotel, Beddgelert.

So, we have emerged from the Vale of Ffestiniog into another vale — that of the Aber Glaslyn.

Bards' Roll

i. **Y Moelwyn**   Hedd Wyn (1887-1917)

ii. **Y Gorwel**   David Emrys James
   The Oxford Book of Welsh Verse O.U.P. 1983

iii. **Cerdd yr Hen Chwarelwr**   William John Gruffydd
   (1881-1954)   The Oxford Book of Welsh Verse

iv. **Y Moelwyn Mawr a'r Moelwyn Bach**   William Jones
   (1896-1961)   The Oxford Book of Welsh Verse

v. **Afon**   Ieuan Jones,   Dyffryn Ardudwy

vi. **Yr Hen Felin**   Monallt   Llyfrfa'r M.C.
   Caernarfon 1969

vii. **Y Ffin**   J Rowland Hughes
   Can Deu Ddwy   Gwasg Gee   Dinbych 1982

viii. **Y Coedwigwr**   Monallt   Llyfrfa'r M.C.

ix. **Gorwel**   Ieuan Jones,   Dyffryn Ardudwy

x. **Hwyrnos**   J Rowland Hughes   Can Neu Ddwy

xi. **Y Ffin**   J Rowland Hughes   Can Neu Ddwy

xii. **Blodau'r Grug**   Eifion Wyn
   The Oxford Book of Welsh Verse

xiii. **Porthmadog**   Ieuan Jones   Dyffryn Ardudwy

Bibliography

Winson, J., *The Little Wonder,* Ffestiniog Railway Company and Michael Joseph, 1975

Nash-Williams, V.E., Jarrett, M.G., *The Roman Frontier in Wales,* University of Wales Press, Cardiff 1969

Jones, A., *A History of Gruffydd ap Cynan,* University of Manchester Press, 1910

Roberts, J.H., *Cerddi Monallt,* Llyfrfa'r M.C., Caernarfon 1969

Rowland Hughes, J., *Can Neu Ddwy,* Gwasg Gee, Dinbych 1982

Parry, T., (editor), *The Oxford Book of Welsh Verse,* O.U.P. 1983

Jones, I., *Poems*

Ordnance Survey publications

Acknowledgements

For information when preparing material for this publication the author wishes to thank the following:

Mr Evan Vaughan Jones, Meiriondy, Penrhyndeudraeth.

Mr Geraint Lloyd Jones, Llwyn Hudol, Penrhyndeudraeth.

Mr Albert Humphreys, Penrhyndeudraeth

Mr R.D. Morgan, conductor of The Royal Oakley Band, Blaenau Festiniog.

Mr R.D. Jones, publicity officer, Côr Meibion y Moelwyn, Blaenau Ffestiniog.

Mr Arthur L. Davies, secretary, Côr Meibion y Brythoniaid, Blaenau Ffestiniog.

PUB WALKS
IN THE
NEW FOREST

Other "pub walking" books
"Pub Walks in Dorset"
"Forty More Pub Walks in Dorset"
"Pub Walks in Hampshire & the I.O.W."
"Pub Walks in West Sussex"
"Pub Walks in East Sussex"
"Pub Walks in Devon"
"Pub Walks in Cornwall"
"Pub Walks in Kent"

1st Edition – published March 1996.

© Power Publications 1996

ISBN 1 898073 10 4

Publisher's Note
Whilst every care has been taken to ensure that all the information given in this book is correct at the time of going to print neither the publishers nor the printers can accept any responsibility for any inaccuracies.

Power Publications
1 Clayford Avenue, Ferndown
Dorset BH22 9PQ

Photographs and line drawings: Mike Power
Printed by Pardy & Son (Printers) Ltd., Ringwood, Hampshire
Front cover: The Royal Oak, Fritham

Introduction

Hunting has always been the sport of kings none more so than the Norman Kings who in 1079 proclaimed the area as the new hunting area of William the Conqueror to be known as "Nova Foresta".

Today the Forest covers an area of 148 square miles and consists of many diverse landscapes. Up until 1482 there were no inclosures but many now exist and were necessary to protect the growth of young trees. Apart from approximately 30,000 acres of woodland; vast areas of open heath, grass lands, bogs or valley mires and gorse occupy a further 93,000 acres. In January 1992, the government recognized the importance of the New Forest by proposing a status equivalent to that of a National Park.

Administration of the Forest is the responsibility of The Verderers Court the second oldest in the land who still sit six times a year in Queens House Lyndhurst. Verderers were once officers of the Crown but still play an important part today working with the planning authorities to ensure no developments take place that would be detrimental to the Forest. They also control and administer the "Rights of Common" and appoint 4 agisters who oversee the welfare of the Commoners animals.

Commoning is a term given to Forest folk who were denied ownership of land but to compensate were given permission to use the Forest for grazing of ponies, cattle, sheep and donkeys. Each year the three hundred or so Commoners turn out more than 3000 ponies and half as many cattle again. It is said that without these four legged grass cutters the Forest would become a wilderness within 20 years. Pannage allows pigs to be turned out in the autumn to consume the acorns which although harmless to pigs can be extremely harmful to ponies. Turbary allows turf to be cut as fuel, Estovers allows cord wood to be taken as fuel and Marl which allows limy clay to be dug.

The Forest has provided a living for many people over the years, timber being the main industry. The Forestry Commission today maintains an annual production of 36,000 cubic metres (36,000 tonnes) of timber. For centuries oak was cut and dispatched to Bucklers Hard and the Naval Dockyard at Portsmouth for shipbuilding. Tourism is now a big source of income and there are a wide choice of camp sites open from the Friday before Easter to the end of September. The main New Forest Tourist Information Centre is located in Lyndhurst and open all year round. Telephone: (01703) 282269.

The Forest is rich in wildlife with many rare species of flora, fauna, birds, reptiles, insects and fungi. The Forest is also home to four types of deer, Red Roe, Sika, Muntjac and Fallow which are by far the most numerous. In certain areas you may well spot a white buck particularly on the walk from the Royal Oak at Bank.

The walks in this book cover all the Forest from Ringwood in the west to Woodfalls in the north, Holbury in the east and Keyhaven in the south. A variety of walks are included that take you across open Forest, beside streams and rivers, along the coast and through dense plantations. Walks vary from 2 to $5\frac{1}{4}$ miles the average distance being about $3\frac{1}{2}$ miles, they are all circular starting and finishing at the pub where rest and refreshment is assured. Following the relaxing of licensing hours many pubs are now open all day seven days a week so in many instances one can amble at leisure assured of refreshment upon ones return.

Each pub listed in this book has been chosen for its own individual charm or accessibility to a good walk; no payment whatsoever is accepted for inclusion. Some are well off the beaten track whilst others occupy prominent roadside positions. There are small traditional Forest inns, large family pubs and many noted for their excellent cuisine. Whilst the majority of pubs have large car parks alternative parking ares are listed at the start of each walk should you not wish to use the facilities of the pub.

Many paths cross the Forest - a lot of them actually made by the animals themselves and as waymarking is almost non existent it is easy to take a wrong path therefore in areas of dense woodland pay special attention to my directions. Should you miss a path don't worry, keep walking and sooner or later you will reach a road and establish your bearing. I always recommend that you carry the relevant Ordnance Survey map as a back up. The three maps in the Landranger series that cover the Forest walks in this book are Nos. 184, 195 and 196.

It has now been proved that walking is extremely good for you and safe provided a few simple rules are observed. Wear suitable clothing, lightweight waterproof trousers are best as many paths can become overgrown especially in summer. A waterproof cagoule is an essential item so too are strong, well treaded waterproof boots. Take care on Forest lanes where there are no pavements and always walk facing the oncoming traffic except on a dangerous right-hand bend. A compass can be useful, so too can a torch if walking in the evening. I always carry a stick: it is ideal for clearing brambles and overgrown paths, testing the stability of the ground ahead and most important, it can be waved in the air if necessary to deter animals. To play your part in ensuring the

Forest's future observe strictly the 40 MPH signs staying well under if possible especially at night where animals tend to congregate on the roads and under arches. The sad facts are that each year some 150 animals are killed. Do not feed the animals and keep children well away from the ponies and donkeys they are wild and will often kick out if approached from behind especially mares in foal. Try to keep dogs on a lead and under control at all times. Be careful when discarding matches or cigarettes especially during the summer. Respect the rules of the Forest; close all gates behind you, keep to the paths across farm land, take all litter home and do not pick or dig up wild flowers or protected fungi.

THE NEW FOREST DISTRICT

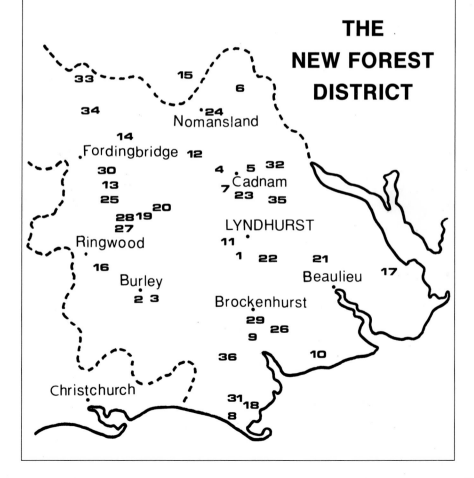

33

15

6

34

•24
Nomansland

14
.Fordingbridge 12

30   4 . 5 **32**
13   7.Cadnam
25   23   35
     20
28 19
27   LYNDHURST
.Ringwood   11

16   1   22   21
  Burley   Beaulieu   **17**
  2 3
        Brockenhurst
          29
          9   26

       36   10

.Christchurch
          31 18
          8

The Oak Inn, Bank

Recently restored this lovely historic inn dates from 1719 when it is said a tunnel linked nearby Queens House in Lyndhurst. Often missed by motorists this attractive pub, very popular with walkers, is sited in a beautiful area of the Forest just minutes from the busy A35. Cattle and horses regularly stand in the shade of the front porch which leads directly into the low beamed open plan bar attractively decorated in green above part wood panelled walls. Rustic furniture neatly positioned on the bare boarded floor consists of scrubbed wooden tables, a mix of chairs and unusual bar stools adapted from milk churns. An attractive feature is the wooden and tile fireplace housing a warm log winter fire. There is additional seating in the small rear garden.

A choice of four real ales is the norm in this freehouse which presently are Ringwood Best, Flowers Original, Old Peculier and Pendragon from the Hampshire Brewery.

Food is available lunch times and from 6.30 p.m. till 9.30 p.m. Listed in the menu are a selection of meals from the chargrill, a bowl of hot chilli, chicken Kiev, crispy coated Camembert and traditional steak and kidney pie plus a couple of fish dishes like lemon sole 'Classico' and king prawns cooked in garlic butter. The substantial snack list includes 'Oak' door step sandwiches, filled jacket potatoes and forester's lunch. Children have a choice of three meals as do vegetarians. A few specials listed daily on the blackboard might include chicken and sweet corn soup, beef and pepper casserole, half a pint of oak smoked shell on prawns and potato skins filled with prawns and asparagus.

Weekday opening times are from 11 a.m. till 3 p.m. and 6 p.m. till 11 p.m. Summertime all day Saturday and Sunday from 12 noon.

Well behaved children and dogs are equally welcome.

Telephone: (01703) 282350.

Bank is signed from the A35 just south from Lyndhurst.

Approx. distance of walk: 3½ miles. OS Map No. 195 SU 287/073.

Park at the front of the pub or in the lane.

A most enjoyable walk along Forest paths, across streams and through dense woodland. White deer can sometimes be seen in an inclosure towards the end of the walk. Whilst mostly good underfoot strong waterproof footwear is recommended in the winter.

1. Leave the pub and turn left along the metalled road until you reach the sign for Gritnam. Turn immediately right through the half wooden gate and walk down towards the stream turning left into the clearing. When you reach the track keep straight ahead uphill onto the track passing the water installation on the right.

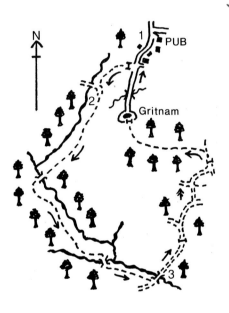

2. It is a fairly long well defined track passing between many fallen trees before reaching the stream. Cross the bridge to the far bank and turn left. Maintain your direction along this often ill-defined path, always keeping close to the stream, until you eventually reach a wooden vehicle bridge. Cross over and turn left following the well defined path, past the deer inclosure to meet the gravel track.

3. Turn left, cross the bridge and proceed along the track, pass through the wooden gate and fork right. As you approach the right-hand bend take the grass track on the left, cross the gravel road and keep straight ahead onto the grass track opposite which curves to the right leading to a wooden gate. Enter Furzehill Inclosure keeping to the main but ill-defined track into the trees, bearing left past more fallen trees eventually reaching a half wooden gate at Gritnam. Keep straight ahead on the metalled road, cross the bridge and retrace your steps back to the pub.

The lane leading from Gritnam to Bank

9

Queens Head, Burley

Popular with summer visitors Burley is one of few villages open to Forest wildlife. Ponies, donkeys and cattle roam free and congregate outside the many small gift shops and village centre pub. The Queens Head has been satisfying local thirsts since 1630 but refurbished over the years. The last major renovation saw the demise of the original sunken festival bar; the large carved wooden fire surround however survived and a glass panel in the wall allows one to see the original wall structure. The pub is steeped in history much of it linked to smuggling indeed a smuggler's horse is reputed to be buried near the bar and pistols, coins and guns have been unearthed over the years. Warmed by winter log fires several linked rooms have an assortment of sturdy furniture on part carpeted floors.

This well managed Whitbread pub offers real ale drinkers Boddingtons Bitter plus two others like Flowers Original and Fuller's London Pride.

Hearty homemade pub food, chalked daily above the food servery could include warming soups, deep fried Camembert, a mega mixed grill, breaded chicken Kiev, roast breast of chicken, whole grilled fresh plaice, beef and venison casserole, steak and kidney pudding, various steaks, vegetarian dishes and typical pub grub like ploughman's and jacket potatoes. For the sweet toothed there are puddings such as toffee apple and pecan pie and strawberry gateaux.

From Monday to Saturday the pub is open all day from 11 a.m. till 11 p.m. Sunday 12 noon till 10.30 p.m.

Children and dogs are most welcome.

Telephone: (01425) 403423.

Burley is signed from both the A35 and the A31.

Approx. distance of walk: 2½ miles. OS Map No. 195 SU 212/031.

There is ample parking to the rear of the pub.

A very enjoyable but slightly demanding walk, first along peaceful Forest roads onto Cranes Moor after which an attractive woodland path descends gently back to the village. Some of the paths can be very muddy in winter.

1. Leave the pub and walk up the hill on the pavement crossing the road when you reach the turning on the right towards Moorhill House Hotel. A few steps further ahead fork left and follow the metalled track down through the trees and then uphill. Fork right at the next junction and continue climbing past the hotel and pond on the left, through the single bar gate into the Forest.
2. Keeping fairly close to the boundary of the dwellings on the right follow the undulating path as it winds though the trees (expect it to be muddy in winter). After descending a hill look for a gap in the hedge on the right and follow the path through the narrow strip of trees until you reach the road.
3. Cross into Castle Hill Lane walking up and round past the dwellings turning immediately left onto the path running beside Beacon Cottage, a few paces further on take the path on the right between the trees and

onto the moor. Proceed along this grassy path which runs fairly close to the field boundaries on the right. Keep straight ahead at the fork following the path into the dip climbing steadily up the far bank until you eventually reach the gravel track (Castle Hill Lane) then turn left.
4. Further ahead look for a stile on the right and follow the signed path through attractive woodland and then onto a fenced path between chestnut trees. After crossing two small wooden bridges the path diverts round a field eventually reaching an iron gate allowing access to a private drive and the road.
5. Turn right, and in fifty paces cross over to the small gate and join the path signposted, Village Centre. Leave by the next gate, cross back over the road meandering at will through the pretty village centre back to the pub.

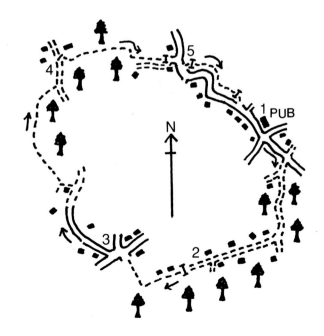

Burley looking east

Burley looking west

The White Buck Inn, Burley

Burley is a popular village for tourists attracted by its many small gift shops and the numerous animals that roam free through its streets, it also boasts two good pubs, The Queens Head in the centre and, hidden away adjacent to the golf club, the large White Buck Inn. A popular venue for horse riders the pub is set in its own grounds. Beyond the foyer of this freehouse are three, plush carpeted rooms warmed by log fires in winter each with its own view across the large stately lawn filled with picnic benches in summer. There is also a play area for children.

Four real ales regularly featured include Ringwood Best, Wadworth 6X, Fuller's London Pride and Ringwood 49er.

Food is served between 12 noon and 2 p.m. and from 7 p.m. till 10 p.m. The bar menu is posted on the blackboard and changes according to what is in season. Apart from freshly made soup, sandwiches, ploughman's and basket meals the choice might range between an oak smoked fillet of trout, pate, a pint of prawns or hot chilli wings with sour cream. There are meals for children, usually a curry, pasta meals of lasagne and tagliatelle, vegetarian macaroni cheese and spinach and cheese quiche plus fish dishes such as poached fresh salmon and grilled local trout. Other meals might be mushroom and Guinness pie, an oak smoked platter of fish and meat, smoked haddock and prawn mornay salad and chargrilled steaks.

Weekday opening times are from 11 a.m. till 2.30 p.m. (Saturday 3 p.m.) and 6 p.m. till 11 p.m.

Children and dogs are both equally welcome.

Overnight accommodation is available offering a choice of 8 double and twin en suite rooms and 1 double non en suite room.

Telephone: (01425) 402264.

Walk No. 3

Burley is signed midway between the A31 and the A35. The White Buck Inn is signed east of the village at the road junction.

Approx. distance of walk: 3¾ miles. OS Map No. 195 SU 224/028.

Park in the lane or the signed parking area nearby.

A very enjoyable walk ideal for all the family along peaceful lanes, on field and Forest paths and gravel tracks. Although fairly level and sound underfoot winter walkers would be well advised to wear strong waterproof footwear.

1. From the pub turn right and then left into Bisterne Close. Carry on along the lane, past many lovely dwellings, and after rounding the bend and passing the post box look for a short gravel driveway on the right, opposite the pond. Walk down to join the narrow track passing through holly trees onto open heath. Keep straight ahead on the wide grass path across a damp area to the stream. Walk over the bridge and bear left skirting the wood, cross the ditch and continue in the same direction until you reach the track beside the inclosure then turn left. Keeping close to the fence maintain direction eventually reaching the lane by the half gate then turn right.

2. After passing a few dwellings you will see a signed footpath on the left. Pass through the gate onto the track, through a second gate and into the field. Keep straight ahead to the stiles then walk down to the wooden bridge, over a concrete bridge and make for the stile opposite. Bear right through the trees turning left upon reaching the gravel drive.

3. Walk across the grass towards the black and white house opposite and head up the track, out into the lane turning right. In 30 paces fork left into Church Lane then left again. Make one last left turn when you reach the golf course walking back to the pub.

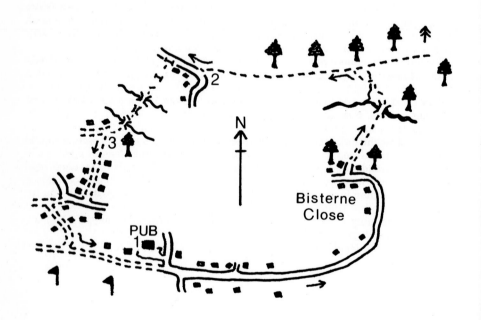

14

The Green Dragon, Brook

Dating from the 15th century this delightful thatched pub, once a wheelwrights and coffin makers premises, first became an ale house some 200 years ago. Recent refurbishment has in no way spoilt what is still essentially a very good local. The warm and cosy 'Tack Room' has a low beamed ceiling, red brick and tiled floors and a large refractory table with pew seating in front of an enormous inglenook fireplace. Similar in appearance the adjoining bar allows access to a very attractive dining room, pretty beer garden and play area for children.

The pub is a freehouse offering a choice of at least four real ales which presently include Flowers Original, Ringwood 49er, Boddingtons Bitter and Castle Eden Ale.

Very good home cooked food is served all week from 12 noon till 2.30 p.m. and 6.30 p.m. (7 p.m. Sunday) till 9.30 p.m. (9 p.m. Sunday). In addition to jacket potatoes, traditional ploughman's and sandwiches specials, chalked daily on the blackboard might include a tasty soup, steak and kidney pudding, and ham and mushroom pie. 'Green Dragon' brunch consists of sausage, bacon, egg, mushrooms, fried bread, black pudding and grilled tomatoes. Curry Club evenings held during the week invite diners to enjoy dishes like curried chicken with cashew nuts, lamb roughan josh and vegetable masala. There is also a separate menu for children.

Weekday opening times are from 10 a.m. till 3 p.m. and 6.30 p.m. till 9.30 p.m. Children and dogs are welcome both in the pub and the garden.

Telephone: (01703) 813359.

Walk No. 4

Brook is signed from the Cadnam roundabout at the junction of the M27 and A31.

Approx. distance of walk: 3½ miles. OS Map No. 195 SU 273/141.

Park at the front or in the car park at the rear of the pub.

A most enjoyable walk at first along an attractive footpath leading to peaceful Forest roads returning through Bignell Wood. The going is generally good underfoot and the absence of stiles makes it an ideal walk for all members of the family. For a longer walk one can link with the Canterton walk on page 24.

1. Leave the pub turning right, over the bridge then cross the road to join the signed path close to the entrance to the large house. The very attractive sunken path passes between bluebell woods and the golf course before reaching a gate at the far end allowing access to the lane.
2. Turn right and proceed along this very peaceful Forest road flanked by parkland on the left and wild flower filled hedgerows beneath a tree canopy. The lane arcs around farm land before reaching a T junction at which point turn right. Cross the ford (or the bridge) and continue following the lane ahead until you eventually reach the road at Wittensford then turn left.
3. Cross over walking to a point just past the road sign (indicating a left-hand bend) and enter Bignell Wood (not signed). Poorly defined at first the path soon becomes more evident the further on you walk. After entering a clearing fork right between holly bushes passing a timbered house on the right. Yomp the ditch, and a few steps further on fork left onto the established track. Cross the fallen tree (if still in place) and keep walking until you reach a narrow cross track then turn right. Walk down and cross the ditch to rejoin the path. Keep straight ahead climbing the bank and follow the path which winds to the left across an area of grass to meet the gravel track. (To link with the Canterton Walk turn left). Turn right, walk past the dwellings, up to the road making one last left turn back to the pub.

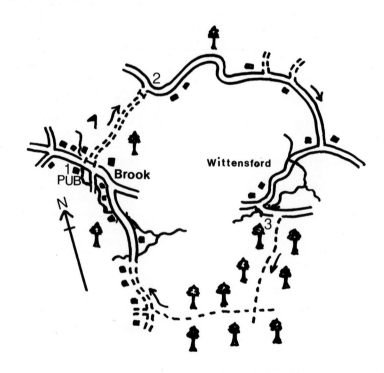

Coalmeer Gutter, Wittensford

Wittensford, Brook

Footpath from Copythorne Common, Cadnam

The White Hart, Cadnam

Recently renovated and attractively refurbished The White Hart has a mix of comfortable chairs and sturdy tables on the bare boarded and quarry tiled floor of the main bar heated by a wood stove set in a large brick fireplace. Close by a selection of choice whiskeys are displayed in a china cabinet behind which there are tables near the bar and more in a small pretty dining room overlooking the sunny front terrace. There is an attractive beer garden, play area for children and skittle alley.

Personally run by the Emberley family the highest of pub traditions are being maintained. Presently four well conditioned real ales are dispensed by hand pump, Flowers Original, Wadworth 6X, Morland Old Speckled Hen and King & Barnes Sussex Bitter.

"Haggard and thin we staggered in happy and stout we staggered out" an apt rhyme for this excellent pub which serves very good and imaginative food up until 2 p.m. at lunch times and 9.30 p.m. in the evening (9 p.m. on Sunday). From the set menu one can choose from a range of starters such as deep fried Brie in beer batter with apricot sauce, air dried duck with a balsamic dressing, or chicken and spring onion satay in peanut sauce. Main meals include fresh Toulouse sausages with a red wine and garlic sauce, gigot of lamb with cherry and almond sauce, venison cutlets served with a sloe and juniper sauce, a pasta dish and the curry of the day. Vegetarians can choose between mushroom stroganoff and leek and spinach strudel with Madeira sauce. Imaginative specials range from a simple chicken and bacon open sandwich to rabbit with spinach and bacon, veal T bone with a Marsala sauce, roast wood pigeon breast and rump of venison roasted with shallots and garlic.

Weekday opening times are from 11 a.m. till 3 p.m. and again from 6 p.m. till 11 p.m.

Both children and dogs are welcome away from the bar.

Telephone: (01703) 812277.

Walk No. 5

Pub sited on the A31 just north of the Cadnam roundabout.

Approx. distance of walk: 3 miles. OS Map No. 196 SU 296/136.

There is a large car park at the front and a smaller one at the rear together with ample street parking.

Apart from occasional noise intrusion from the motorway this is a pleasant easy walk at first along the road to Bunker Hill (with the option of following marked walks on Copythorne Common) returning along peaceful Forest roads beside Cadnam Green.

1. From the front of the pub turn left or from the rear of the pub turn right into Old Romsey Road, walk down to the main road and then turn left. Further on turn left into Newbridge Road signposted, Newbridge ¾. Turn left at the junction, pass under the motorway and immediately turn right onto the gravel track.

2. Although not an official 'right of way' the owners allow access to the waymarked paths. Pass through a second gate walking until you reach a stile on the left then cross onto the wide grass track following it into the woods ahead. Reach the stile beside the gate on the far side and join the narrow footpath running behind the dwelling leading down to the lane and turn right.

3. Take the next left and left again at the road junction keeping to the narrow Forest road beside Cadnam Green. After about a mile take the turning left, pass under the motorway then next left back to the pub.

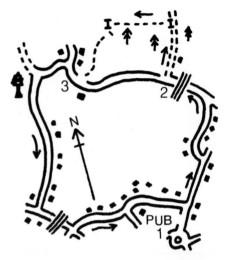

Cadnam Green

Rockford Green

Fritham

Rockingham Arms, Canada

Known locally as the 'Rock' and named after the local brick works, this 19th century family run inn, peacefully situated on the northern edge of the Forest, was built originally as a chapel but never used for worship.

Accommodation comprises two bars. The Forest and Pool Room, larger than the lounge which extends to accommodate a pew seated family area and has a stone floor at the bar and an open fireplace. Diners though may prefer to sit in the restaurant overlooking the rear lawns and Forest beyond where there is a play area for children and a pretty vine covered beer garden.

This friendly well run freehouse offers a good choice of real ales which, apart from Wadworth 6X offers up to a further five selected from at least 50. Beers such as Bunces Old Smokey, Fuller's London Pride, Hard Tackle and Morland Old Speckled Hen to name but a few.

Food is available from 12 noon and includes a full range of bar snacks plus blackboard specials such as roast lamb, breaded trout with almonds and aubergine and potato moussaka. From the set menu one can order soup or Japanese prawns, followed by homemade dishes of venison pie, beef ale and mushroom pie, Mexican chilli and beef curry. 'Canadian Brunch' consists of bacon, sausage, fried egg, tomato and mushrooms served with either hash browns or pancakes with maple syrup. Order 'Salmon Shanti' if you enjoy salmon and broccoli in a creamy white sauce flavoured with dill, breaded and deep fried. Additional choice from the á la carte restaurant menu lists clam chowder or avocado pear filled with choice crab and shrimp glazed with Marie Rose sauce. Steaks can be ordered with a choice of mouth watering sauces such as 'Canadienne' which comes topped with demerara sugar and rye whisky. The sweet specialities are freshly made pancakes with maple syrup.

Weekday opening times are from 11.30 a.m. till 2.30 p.m. and 6 p.m. till 11 p.m.

Children and dogs are both equally welcome inside and out.

Telephone: (01794) 322473.

Canada is signed from the A36 Salisbury to Southampton road at West Wellow.

Approx. distance of walk: 3¼ miles. OS Map No. 184 SU 287/179.

Ample parking at the rear, the front and in the lane outside.

A short but nevertheless very enjoyable, level walk across Canada and Penn Commons. The going is good underfoot and there are no stiles making it ideal for all members of the family.

1. Leave the pub and turn right and right again at the bend. Further on enter the Forest and keep straight ahead across the grass following the rutted track (not very well defined) as it snakes across open Forest towards distant woods. Before drawing level with the trees bear left across the scrub and continue walking to the left, skirting the edge of the woods until you reach the dirt path at which point turn right, cross both plank bridges maintaining your direction. The path eventually widens to a gravel track and is metalled after passing Paddock

Cottage. Follow the road round the bend then cut left across the green turning left to join the road.

2. Keep walking beside Penn Common turning left when you reach the wide gravel track as it first bears right, past several dwellings, and then round to the left past more large country properties. Ignore your entry point to the common but continue ahead for a short distance finally reaching a gate marked, "entrance to the Rockingham Arms".

23

Sir Walter Tyrrell, Rufus Stone, Canterton

Popular with tourists this interesting pub occupies a sunny open position in a peaceful area of the Forest named, it is said, after the alleged assassin of King William, nick-named Rufus after his long red hair. Nearby "Rufus Stone", a monument erected in 1745 but later covered with an iron protector, marks the spot where on August 2 1100 he is reputed to have met his death whilst hunting.

Served by a central bar a series of open plan rooms are heated by winter fires. Lots of interesting paraphernalia and hop flowers adorn the wooden walls and ceilings. There is a very attractive dining room and a cool summer patio overlooking the garden where there is a small shop located and excellent facilities for children including toddlers toys.

This well managed pub offers three real ales Directors Bitter, Ruddles County and Courage Best.

Food is available all day during May through till the end of August otherwise from 12 noon till 2 p.m. and 6 p.m. till 9 p.m. Ordered from the servery the set menu includes starters like crispy potato skins and Italio bake - freshly cooked tagliatelle served in a creamy cheese sauce with julienne of smoked salmon followed by hot platters of steak, mushroom and ale pie and butterfly chicken. Daily blackboard specials might include fresh fish and mussels or an Oriental stir fry. A good range of sandwiches, jacket potatoes and ploughman's are also available as well as vegetarian meals such as mushroom stroganoff and Raj vegetable curry. The more comprehensive a la carte menu lists roast duckling, and a seven bone rack of lamb.

Presently the pub is open all day between May and August otherwise Monday to Friday from 11 a.m. till 2.30 p.m. and 6 p.m. till 11 p.m. Open all day Saturday and Sunday.

The Sir Walter Tyrrell is a family pub and welcomes children throughout. There is no objection to dogs on a lead in the pub but not in the garden.

Telephone: (01703) 813170.

Rufus Stone is signed from the northern carriageway of the A31 just south of the M27.

Approx. distance of walk: 3½ miles. OS Map No. 195 SU 268/127.

Park in the pub car park, in the road or preferably in the Rufus Stone car park.

A very enjoyable walk across open grassland, along bridleways and through dense woodland. Strong waterproof footwear is to be recommended in the winter. For a longer walk you can link with the Brook walk on page 16

1. Bearing slightly right leave the pub and head across the grass opposite yomping the occasional ditch keeping close to the inclosure on the right. Cross Coalmeer Gutter by means of the improvised stone block bridge and climb the track ahead. Cross the plank bridge and bear left along the wide grassy track rising through the trees eventually meeting a gravel road leading into King's Garn Gutter Inclosure on the right.

2. Pass through the gate and follow the wide track round to the left. Although not an official 'right of way' it is one of many permissible paths in the Forest. Upon reaching the junction of five tracks peel off to the right down the grass track turning right onto the gravel track and left at the next track.

3. Walk down to the gate, exit through onto the golf course and bear right carefully walking across the fairway down to the plank bridge crossing King's Garn Gutter

and a second plank bridge. Pick up the track beyond beside the field boundary and follow it round and out into the lane.

4. Keep straight ahead walking downhill to the ford, cross by the footbridge turning left onto the bridleway (just before the letterbox) which soon deteriorates into an attractive but often muddy track. An alternative dry path has been established by walkers on the left bank. Further on cross the bridge over Coalmeer Gutter for the second time and walk up the track, past the dwellings to the gravel lane then turn right, (to join the Brook walk turn left).

5. Walk past the last of the dwellings, pass through the half wooden gate and onto the Forest. Round the hedge boundary at the bottom, cross the ditch and keep straight ahead always in sight of the boundary on the right. Eventually you will see a thatched cottage after which turn right along the short grass track and return to the pub.

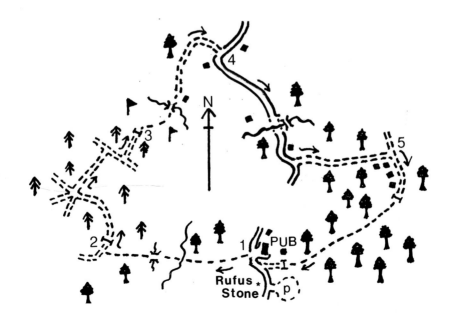

Rufus Stone

View of the I.O.W. from the coast path at Downton

The Royal Oak, Downton

Dating back to 1695 The Royal Oak is a traditional pub run by the same family for the past 136 years.

A series of interconnected low beamed rooms, one reserved exclusively for non-smokers, each have their own open fire. Many old farm implements and lots of brightly shining regalia adorn the walls whilst comfortable furnishings are in the country style. There are iron tables and chairs in the flower filled covered side patio, picnic benches in the rear beer garden and a play area for children. The pub is beautifully kept inside and out resplendent in summer with many colourful flower filled tubs and hanging baskets.

The well stocked bar includes three regular real ales Wadworth 6X, Ringwood Best Bitter and Flowers Original plus a small selection of country wines.

Food times are from 12 noon till 2 p.m. and 6.30 p.m. till 9 p.m. (9.30 p.m. Friday and Saturday). Bar snacks include soup of the day, smoked mackerel, tropical toast - a thick slice of gammon topped with pineapple and toasted cheese, assorted jacket potatoes, prawn and garlic delight, farmers choice ploughman's and sandwiches followed by steak pie, sweet and sour pork, fisherman's hot pot and beef lasagne. For vegetarians there is a curry, macaroni and broccoli cheese bake and a homemade country pancake filled with tomatoes, mushrooms and onions topped with cheese sauce. Daily specials might include coq au vin with new potatoes. Puddings range from cherry pancakes topped with ice cream to apple pie with custard.

Weekday opening times are from 11.30 a.m. till 2.30 p.m.(3 p.m. Saturday) and 6.30 p.m. till 11 p.m. Sunday 12 noon till 3 p.m. and 7 p.m. till 10.30 p.m.

Children and dogs in the garden only.

Telephone: (01590) 642297.

Walk No. 8

Pub located at the crossroads in Downton on the main A337 Christchurch to Lymington Road.

Approx. distance of walk: 2¾ miles. OS Map No. 195 SZ 268/935.

Leave your car in the rear car park or preferably in the lay-by by the telephone box.

A short but extremely enjoyable walk ideal for all members of the family through attractive woodland, along a very scenic coastal path, across farm land returning along a path beside a bluebell wood. After a muddy start the going is mostly good underfoot.

1. From the pub turn left walking the short distance before reaching the fingerpost just beyond the lay-by. It directs you onto a field path leading to the woods on the far side after which a well trodden path descends gently through attractive woodland to a bridge. Cross the Danes Stream and follow the path ahead up a rather boggy incline and through a rhododendron arch into a coniferous wood at the top. Keep straight ahead onto the gravel track walking down to meet the road.

2. Cross over to the kissing gate and path opposite keeping to the well marked diversion through the golf course eventually reaching the cliff edge.

3. Turn left (heeding the warning notices) and continue along the path enjoying splendid views across the water to the Needles and the Isle of Wight. When you reach an old war fortification follow the signed path inland which leads you up to a car park then turn right into the road and carefully cross to the signed footpath opposite.

4. Enter the field and head for the crossing point and bridge opposite, climb the bank to the fence turning left, and after reaching the crossing point join the path skirting the bluebell wood. At the far crossing point turn right along the field boundary to the track, keep straight ahead to the stile, out into the lane and turn left back to the pub.

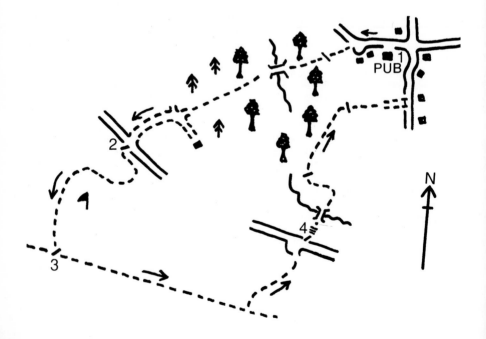

28

Hare & Hounds, Durnstown

Daily papers, neatly positioned on a heavy pine table, await you upon entering the main bar of this popular pub last renovated as recently as 1995. There are open fireplaces, one white painted brick another part wood panelled, rugs on the floor and a part boarded and beamed ceiling. There is a separate dining room at one end of the pub and a comfortable lounge the other where assorted furniture generally consists of comfortable armchairs, pew seats, settles and a mix of tables and chairs. Nautical regalia is displayed around the walls together with old photographs. Picnic benches are neatly positioned on the front terrace.

The pub offers a choice of four real ales Ringwood Best, Wadworth 6X, Flowers Original and Fuller's London Pride.

The menu is chalked on the blackboard and includes sandwiches and very good ploughman's which come with a choice of rind cheeses, walnut breads, homemade coleslaw, onions, chutney and salad. Also homemade soup of the day, bacon baguettes, homemade fish pie made with chunks of cod and fresh salmon, prawns and leeks, homemade steak and kidney cooked in Guinness and home cooked ham, egg and chips. There is a separate menu for children and a vegetarian choice. Sweets range from homemade bread and butter pudding and fruit crumble to coffee and walnut profiteroles and a terra-cotta ice cream pot (you keep the pot). The more comprehensive menu, chalked on the blackboard in the dining room, lists smoked salmon with a melon and kiwi sorbet and fish soup followed by game hen in a mild orange sauce with wild rice, rabbit casserole with a herb crust, braised oxtail in red wine and baked whole sea bass in a beurre blanc with Pernod.

Weekday opening times are from 11 a.m. till 3 p.m. and 6 p.m. till 11 p.m.

There is a play area and room for children.

Telephone: (01590) 682404

Walk No. 9

Pub located at Durnstown on the B3055.

Approx. distance of walk: 4 miles. OS Maps Nos. 195 & 196 SZ 283/987.

Park at the pub or in one of the roads opposite.

A thoroughly enjoyable walk across open Forest on sandy paths, gravel tracks and along a disused railway line. It is good underfoot and their are no stiles making it an ideal family walk.

1. leave the pub and turn right walking as far as the small wooden gate on the right. Go through onto the grass, past the war memorial and along the lane. Keep straight ahead at the junction with Coombe Lane, past the turning for Lymington arcing left into Shirley Holms. (After passing the allotments you can pick up the path on the Forest edge and avoid the road). Keep to the grass verge following the lane until you reach the point where it bears right.
2. Turn left here onto the small sandy path which heads downhill in line with overhead cables. Take care as deep gullies have been carved by water erosion. Reach the stream at the bottom, cross the bridge and turn left walking fairly close to the stream. Muddy at first the path soon widens and becomes more obvious before reaching the road.
3. Walk straight across onto the wide grass area ahead which soon narrows to a dirt

path winding its way across the heath eventually reaching the Brockenhurst road. Walk straight across and join the footpath opposite, go under the railway arch and head across the heath turning left onto the gravel drive. Keep walking, and when you reach the dwelling turn left to join the old railway line.
4. Good underfoot the area is now abundant with wildlife and a good place to find fungi in the autumn, the taking of small quanities for your own immediate consumption is acceptable. Walk as far as the gap then go down the bank to the track and turn left. Walk up to the road and straight across following the sandy path as it bears left down across the heath. Wider in places than others it eventually leads to a small bridge over the railway line and a path beyond which leads to the pub.

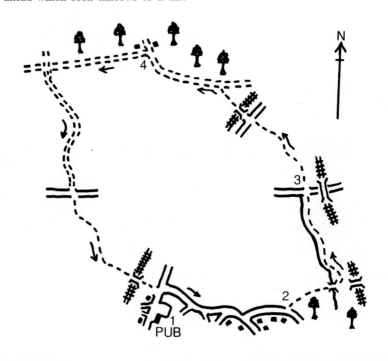

Boletus erythropus (ceps) photographed during the walk from Durnstown

Heathland path close to Beaulieu Road Pub

East End Arms, East End

One of few traditional Forest inns the unpretentious East End Arms was built as a pub in 1825. The original stone floor still remains in the public bar whilst the more comfortable lounge has a piano beside the fireplace and a collection of stag horns and old photographs displayed on the walls. Furnishings consist of pine tables and chairs and both bars are heated by open winter fires. There is a small beer garden at the side with picnic benches.

Being a freehouse the choice of real ales changes regularly. Dispensed straight from the wood there could be any number which might include Ringwood 49er and Thumper, Adnams Broadside Pendragon Ale and Morland Old Speckled Hen.

Food is served from 12 noon till 2 p.m. and 6.30 p.m. till 9 p.m. Chalked on the blackboard the selection of snacks on my last visit included half a pint of prawns, garlic bread with various toppings, filled jacket potatoes, 'East End' ploughman's and homemade pigeon pate, followed by sausage, egg and chips, homemade turkey and bean stew, beef curry, hot chilli, chicken tikka, a choice of roasts and faggots with bubble and squeak and gravy plus a vegetarian dish. East End pies are made by a strange little old lady down the road (there words not mine) and contain pigeon, steak and Guinness, steak and kidney and game and leek. For the sweet toothed there are chocolate and treacle puddings.

Opening times are from 11.30 a.m. till 3 p.m. (2.30 p.m. Thursday and Friday) and from 6 p.m. till 11 p.m.

Dogs are welcome but children are not allowed in the bars after 7.30.p.m.

Telephone: (01590) 65223.

East End Arms is signed from Bucklers Hard and from the B3054 Beaulieu to Lymington Road.

Approx. distance of walk: 2½ miles. OS Map No. 196 SZ 363/967.

Park on the front forecourt or in the lay-by opposite.

A short but nevertheless very enjoyable walk ideal for all the family across level farm land and through attractive woodland.

1. Leave the pub and turn left walking along the lane soon to reach a signed footpath on the right. Cross the stiles into the field and turn right. Keeping close to the hedge on the right make your way across to the stile and into the field ahead. Passing between fenced fields the grass covered path is wide and good underfoot. Reach the lane and turn right.
2. Follow the lane past the dwellings until you reach a signed footpath on the right. Cross into the field and keep straight ahead walking close to the boundary on the left. Further on cross the plank bridge and the stile and enter the adjoining field turning right. Leave by the stile on the far side.

3. Turn left into the lane and almost immediately go over the stile into the field on the right. Make your way over to the plank bridge and bear right through the trees to the stile, cross over onto the track and turn right walking almost the length of this very attractive beech and hazel coppice.
4. Eventually when you reach open farm land on the left turn immediately right onto The Solent Way (signed). The wide grass track leads to a stile and field path from where there are good views across the Solent to the Isle of Wight. After negotiating a couple more stiles reach the kissing gate and turn right into the lane back to the pub.

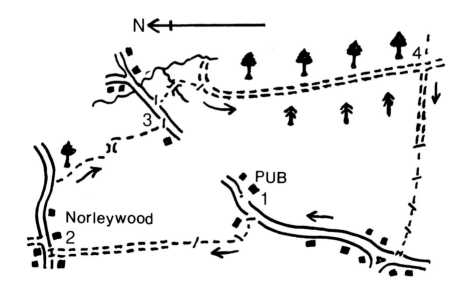

The sketch maps in this book are not necessarily to scale but have been drawn to show the maximum amount of detail.

The New Forest Inn, Emery Down

In the eighteenth century squatters claimed the land from the King upon which this attractive pub now stands selling beer from a caravan. The caravan itself now forms all of the front porch and can also be seen forming a bar wall.

Enlarged over the years this attractive Forest inn offers the modern traveller a warm welcome in a relaxed atmosphere. Part panelled walls, beamed ceilings and assorted furnishings characterize the three cosy rooms heated by warm winter log fires. There is a barbecue and picnic benches on the sunny back lawn.

This pub is a Whitbread Wayside Inn offering five real ales which presently include Gales HSB, Strong Country Bitter, Flowers Original, Boddingtons Bitter and Greene King Abbot Ale.

Imaginative home cooked food is served all week from 12 noon till 9.30 p.m. (9 p.m. Sunday) catering for children and vegetarians alike. Apart from homemade soup, sandwiches and ploughman's the printed menu lists roast pheasant in bacon, mushroom and red wine sauce, fillet of pork in a cashew nut and cream sauce and breast of duck with ginger, honey and spring onion sauce. More dishes on the specials board might include roast topside of beef in a Claret sauce, sauteed beef with Stilton and walnuts, a fresh salmon salad, Foresters mixed grill, wild rabbit in mustard sauce, rack of lamb in port wine sauce, sauteed lamb in raspberry sauce and fried liver in a Stilton sauce. Typical sweets are fresh strawberry pavlova and homemade peach and strawberry cheese cake.

The inn is open all day every day from 11 a.m. till 11 p.m. Sunday 12 noon till 10.30 p.m.

Well behaved children and dogs are both equally welcome.

For those requiring accommodation there are four en suite double rooms.

Telephone. (01703) 282329.

Emery Down is signed from the A35 west of Lyndhurst.

Approx. distance of walk: 2½ miles. OS Map No. 195 SU 286/085.

Park at the front of the inn or at the side on the Fritham road.

A short but very enjoyable woodland walk ideal for a dry summer's day.

1. Cross the road and turn left walking up and then downhill passing several dwellings before reaching a gravel track on the left signposted, Crown Wood Stables. Thirty paces along the drive bear left across the grass, join a dirt path and turn right. Further down when you reach a clump of birch trees take the path on the left downhill through a holly and beech tree thicket. After entering an area of grass fork left onto a fairly wide track which passes through a mature oak and beech wood. Further on when the path reaches an area of damp grassland (can be very muddy in the winter) keep straight ahead across the ditch then along a gully which leads up to the road.

2. Walk straight across into the trees opposite and bear right to reach a small brook. Step across, and keeping level with the brook, walk for some distance until you eventually reach a small wooden bridge at which point turn left, cross the bridge and follow the path into the trees ahead. Maintain your direction through an open grass area, ignoring the cross track, turning left when you reach the high brick wall.

3. Stay on the main track for some distance. Deer abound here in the dense woods so walk quietly. Cross the bridge and continue walking before reaching the wide cross track at which point turn left following it through the trees, out into the lane turning right back to the pub.

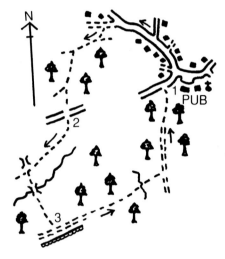

A woodland path near the end of the walk

Royal Oak, Fritham

There are very few original pubs still left in the Forest today but find Fritham and the Royal Oak and you have found one of the best. Situated at the end of a long lane in a remote and peaceful area of the Forest this delightful, genuine part thatched pub is still one of my favourites and apart from an occasional lick of paint has not changed over the years. The simply furnished small front bar is heated in winter by an open fire set in the end wall. The smaller rear bar positively oozes with character enhanced by haphazardly leaning walls, a low closely boarded ceiling and an open fire on a raised bed in a large fireplace. Simple furnishings include a high back wooden settle. Outside there is an aviary and seating in the peaceful side garden.

Resident tenants, Andrew and Eileen Taylor who are the third generation, purchased the pub in 1994 and intend to keep it exactly the way it is. Real ale is still served traditionally straight from the barrel offering a choice of two or three such as Ringwood Bitter, Adnams or Strong Country Bitter.

Food is limited to sandwiches, cockles and crisps etc.

Weekday opening times are from 11 a.m. till 2.30 p.m. (3 p.m. Saturday) and 6 p.m. till 11 p.m. Sunday 12 noon till 3 p.m. and 7.p.m till 10.30 p.m.

Children in garden only. No objection to dogs.

Telephone: (01703) 812606.

Fritham is signed from the northbound carriageway of the A31 at Stoney Cross. If approaching from a northerly direction, take the B3079 and then the B3078.

Approx. distance of walk: 4 miles. OS Map No. 195 SU 232/142.

Park outside the pub or in the signed Forest car park beyond the pub on the left.

A very enjoyable but sometimes muddy walk across open heath and through dense forest. There are no stiles.

1. Leave the pub turning right then turn left onto the gravel track leading to the car park, fork right and right again through the half timber gate following the gravel track down through the woods until you reach the cross track at which point turn left.
2. The wide but often muddy track rises though mixed woodland before reaching a narrow path uphill across the heath between holly trees. Ignore all the side paths but carry on ahead keeping to the path as it bears slightly right. Further on fork left staying on the narrow path until you eventually reach the gravel track.
3. Turn right heading for the inclosure, soon to swing left onto a grass and gravel track. Keep bearing right as you descend towards the inclosure where you will soon find a well defined path leading to the stream at the bottom. Cross both bridges turning left onto

the wide track just before reaching the entrance gate to the inclosure (wet in places during the winter).
4. Keep to the track negotiating the occasional fallen tree but always staying fairly close to the stream on the left. Although ill-defined at first the further on you walk the more obvious the route becomes. There are lots of crab apple trees and well grazed springtime bluebells along the way. After entering a clearing bear left and join the path close to the stream. Maintain direction walking past the inclosure on the right, yomp a small stream and then keep straight ahead across the damp grass area following the path ahead up towards the gate turning left upon reaching the footpath. Make for the stream ahead, cross the bridge and follow the track uphill past the dwellings to the pub.

Pigs set out to pannage at Fritham

Dockens Water, Fritham

Thorns Inclosure, Fritham

The Foresters Arms, Frogham

Peacefully situated The Foresters Arms is a typical village local built around the turn of the century. The main bar has white plastered walls, an open log fire and a thatched roof over the bar. A dartboard is sensibly placed at one end whilst a pool table is located in a room at the back. There is a cosy dining room overlooking the large rear beer garden.

One of the few remaining freehouses in the Forest The Foresters Arms is a mecca for real ale enthusiasts with a choice of least six picked from a constantly changing list. Presently there is Summer Lightning, Boddingtons Bitter, Smiles Best Bitter, Batemans Original, Ringwood Best Bitter, Draught Bass and Abbot Ale. Regular beer festivals are held during the year offering even more choice.

Food is served all week from 12 noon till 2 p.m. and 6.30 p.m. (7 p.m. Sunday) till 10 p.m. (9.30 p.m. Sunday). Daily specials such as mussels poached with garlic, wine and cream and chicken breast with asparagus in a wine and cream sauce supplement the printed menu which includes a choice of starters, fish and chargrills. Also listed are Murphy's steak and mushroom pie, traditional lasagne, homemade quiche, several omelettes, salads, sandwiches and ploughman's plus a daily roast. Vegetarians can choose between vegetable lasagne and leek and potato pie and there is a kiddies menu.

Opening times are from 11 a.m. till 3 p.m. and 6 p.m. till 11 p.m. Open all day Saturday.

Children are welcome away from the bar and every weekend there is a bouncy castle. Dogs are welcome on a lead.

Telephone: (01425) 652294.

Frogham is best reached from Fordingbridge. Take the Stuckton road and follow the signs ignoring all side turnings.

Approx. distance of walk: 4 miles. OS Map No. 195 SU 174/129.

Park in the lane outside or in the car park beside the pub.

A seemingly long but most enjoyable scenic walk across open Forest to the Alderhill Inclosure returning beside Latchmore Brook and passing through the small hamlet of Ogdens. Strong waterproof footwear is recommended on all but dry summer days.

1. From the pub turn left walking to the end of the village, downhill to the sharp left-hand bend and keep straight ahead through the half gate onto the wide forestry track. Keep walking for about a mile and a half over Hampton Ridge until eventually you reach the gate leading into Alderhill Inclosure. For the more adventurous there is a path on the right which leaves the track crossing open heath rejoining it again just before the woods.

2. Pass through the wooden gate and follow the track down to the brook crossing as best you can. The best place is on the left where an area of gravel has accumulated. Keep straight ahead to the gate and turn right onto a sandy path. Although very uneven and boggy in places it is fairly easy to follow running close to the brook on the right. When eventually you reach the track at Ogdens turn right then fork left and left again past the farm buildings turning right onto the track soon to cross the grass on the left where you will find a footbridge over the brook.

3. On the far side bear left, leave the track, round the bend and head up the rise keeping close to the properties on the right. Climbing steadily bear left when you near the top then turn left onto the gravel track. Walk down to meet the lane, turn right and right again at the crossroads back to the pub.

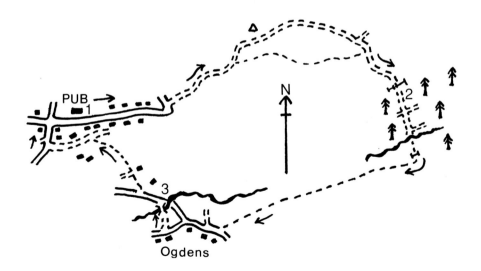

Ogdens

The sketch maps in this book are not necessarily to scale but have been drawn to show the maximum amount of detail.

The Fighting Cocks, Godshill

Overlooking the Forest and popular with tourists from the local caravan park this imposing pub has a white painted and board fronted exterior above a sunny flower filled terrace. Inside one sparsely furnished bar has an open fireplace and rear games room whilst the more comfortable, carpeted through lounge has a large open fireplace and cartwheels suspended from the ceiling.

Three real ales presently available are Flowers Original, Ringwood Best Bitter and Wadworth 6X.

The printed menu lists homemade soup, pate, ploughman's, jacket potatoes, several omelettes and an interesting choice of sandwiches and salads. Other favourite bar meals include homemade steak and kidney pie, chilli, lasagne, ham egg and chips, steaks and smoked haddock and pasta bake with a roast on Sunday. On a recent visit I noted the specials board began with potato wedges with salad garnish, baked jacket potato with curry and chicken masala. Vegetarians would not be disappointed with cheese and broccoli bake served with crusty bread, ricotta cheese and spinach cannelloni or the spinach and mushroom lasagne nor fish eaters with the lemon sole bon femme. Traditional puddings included hot chocolate fudge cake, apple pie and cream and sticky toffee pudding.

Families are welcome and there is no objection to dogs.

Open all year, nearby Sandy Balls Holiday Centre has superbly equipped holiday homes plus camping and touring facilities.

Weekday opening times are from 11 a.m. till 3 p.m. and 6 p.m. till 11 p.m.

Telephone: (01425) 652462.

Pub situated on the B3078 about a mile and a half east of Fordingbridge.

Approx. distance of walk: 3¾ miles. OS map No. 195 SU 177/149.

Ample parking around pub.

A very enjoyable scenic walk across open Forest and farm land, ideal for all the family.

1. Leave the pub and cross the road into the lane opposite signposted, Newgrounds Only. Follow this peaceful undulating lane, past all the dwellings and onto open heath and scrub. Keep close to the field boundary bearing right at the corner, cross Ditchend Brook and walk around the field to pick up the track close to the southern boundary.
2. After passing the entrance to 'Bracken Cottage' join the driveway soon to reach a stile on the right beside a gate. Cross onto the track, walk down to the bridge and turn right. Climb the stile onto the narrow path - springtime host to swathes of pearlwort, bluebells and violets interspersed with yellow calandine. Reach the stile and turn left, cross a second stile into the field and keep straight ahead to the bridge maintaining direction up the field to the stile in the

corner. Bearing slightly right head up the rise to the stiles taking time to look back and enjoy the view. Maintain direction beside the flower filled hedge crossing the stile into the adjoining field, over to the stile on the far side, out into the lane and turn left.
3. Almost immediately cross over into the entrance to Sandy Balls Caravan Park and fork right walking past the visitor centre and Woodside Inn. Further on fork right keeping to the main drive through the park, past Northfield toilet block and up to the stile beside the gate. Cross onto the path and turn left, reach the stile beside the gate and turn right over the stile into the field. Upon reaching the pair of stiles climb into the adjoining field and turn right along the track veering right just before the gate to the stile, go out into the lane and turn right back to the pub.

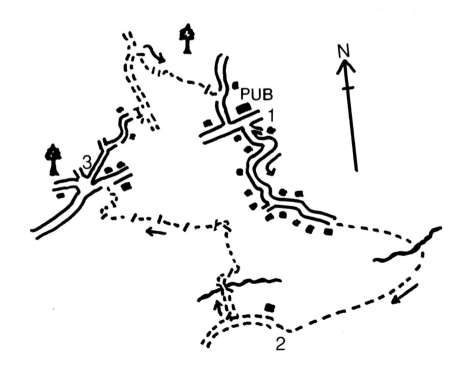

Cuckoo Inn, Hamptworth

Happily within the confines of the Forest there are still a few unspoilt inns. One of my favourites is the charming, thatched Cuckoo Inn at Hamptworth. Built some three hundred years ago it was once the village shop before becoming a pub in the 1930's. Inside one bar serves a series of small cosy simply furnished rooms heated in winter by open fires. Outside there is a swing for children and picnic benches in the sunny, flower filled front garden.

The Inn, a freehouse owned and personally run by Jean and Derek Proudley and Ray, is a mecca for real ale enthusiasts with a constantly changing list of up to nine at any one time. Presently there is Summer Lightning and GFB from the local Hop Back Brewery, Ringwood's Tanglefoot and 49er, Wadworth 6X, Tanglefoot from Hall & Woodhouse, Draught Bass, Bunces Best and Pots Ale. Also Taunton cider.

Food is typical pub fayre consisting of traditional ploughman's with ham or cheese, filled rolls, Cornish pasties and crisps.

Monday to Friday the inn is open from 11.30 a.m. till 2.30 p.m. and again from 6 p.m. till 11 p.m. All day Saturday from 11.30 a.m. till 11 p.m. and Sunday from 12 noon.

There is no objection to either children or dogs in the pub.

Telephone: (01794) 390302.

The most direct route to the pub is from the A36, Southampton to Salisbury road turning south onto the B3079 and then right into Hamptworth Road.

Approx. distance of walk: 5 miles. OS Map No. 184 SU 243/198.

There are two gravel parking areas either side of the road.

Although fairly long this delightful walk, ideal for all members of the family, at first takes you along a peaceful country lane then onto an attractive woodland path to reach Langley Wood Nature Reserve. After enjoying the splendour of this ancient wood a series of field paths provide the route back to the pub.

1. From the pub turn left and then first right towards Nomansland. Follow the lane round to the right, turning right at the next bend. Continue along this peaceful country lane, past a few isolated dwellings and Home Farm on the left and enter the woods. Good underfoot the woodland track soon narrows to a dirt path passing through more attractive woodland later becoming firmer underfoot and then tarred before reaching a small settlement.
2. On the right look for a short track leading to a stile, it is just this side of a black and white timbered building named Merrow. Climb into the field making your way across to the stile behind the telegraph pole and follow the path through the grass and trees, over the bridge and keep straight ahead up the field to the road at the top.
3. Walk straight across to the stile opposite entering Langley Wood Nature Reserve. This ancient wood is rich in wild life including lichens, mosses, woodland plants, insects and birds and five species of deer. Of special interest is the small leafed lime once common in the forests of Southern England. Follow the well trodden path through this most attractive of woods forking right at the first path junction (look for the arrow on the post). Follow the signed path forking left at the next fingerpost into an area of large

oaks above a carpet of spring bluebells. Further on cross the ditch keeping to the path ahead for quite some distance until reaching a cross track at which point turn right and then left into the lane.
4. Shortly re-enter Langley Wood and further ahead fork right keeping to the gully which leads to the golf course. Heeding the warning notice, bear left in the direction of the arrow and keep to the path downhill to the little bridge and then bear left back into the trees joining the rising gravel track. Turn right at the cross track (not the smaller one leading to the golf course) and walk up to the farm, through the gate and across the yard. Almost immediately look for a stile in the hedge on the right.
5. Cross into the field keeping close to the hedge, reach the gate and enter the field on the right turning left. Walk towards the three farm gates passing through the kissing gate entering the field on the right. Cross to the stile on the far side and follow the woodland track down to the bridge and up into the field ahead. Make your way to the hedge at the top turning left, then right and enter the field on the right. Walk down to the stile in the fence, across a couple more stiles, out into the road and turn right back to the pub.

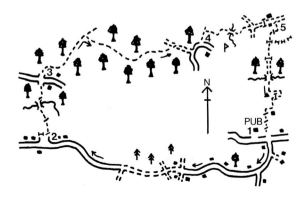

Elm Tree Inn, Hightown, Ringwood

Although having undergone several major renovations this lovely thatched pub has never lost its essential character. Originally two small cosy bars there are now three principal areas. The large comfortably furnished main bar, a smaller bar dominated by a large inglenook fireplace and a small cosy non-smoking room. Above the bare boarded and carpeted floor exposed brick walling supports the partly beamed ceilings. The pub is beautifully kept and efficiently run and on my last visit I was offered a morning paper to read. Adjoining the main pub is a converted barn catering for skittle parties, private functions and conferences. Fresh air lovers may choose to sit in the sunny front garden.

This well run Whitbread tenancy offers a choice of real ales including Wadworth 6X, Flowers Original, Marston's Pedigree, Boddingtons Bitter plus a guest such as Gales HSB and a winter warmer once the evenings draw in.

Pub meals are chalked on the blackboard, the majority of which are homemade. Begin with spicy hot chicken wings, deep fried crispy mushrooms or potato wedges and follow up with grilled supreme of chicken marinated in yoghurt and tikka spices, butterfly breast of garlic chicken, gammon steak and Forest game pie - venison and pheasant topped with puff pastry. The fish choice might be lemon sole 'Classcico' which is breaded and deep fried, breaded seafood platter and local Avon trout. Vegetarians can choose between vegetable and nut lasagne, vegetable moussaka or a nut roast. Daily specials included homemade fisherman's bake - a medley of seafood topped with sliced potato and cheese or homemade chilli.

Children are welcome inside the pub and there is no objection to dogs.

All week the inn is open daily from 11 a.m. till 11 p.m and Sunday from 12 noon till 10.30 p.m.

Telephone: (01425) 472516.

Hightown is signposted from the A31 north of Ringwood.

Approx. distance of walk: $2\frac{1}{2}$ miles. OS Map No. 195 SU 163/049.

Park at the front or rear of the pub, in the small lay-by outside or in Crow Lane opposite.

Although just within earshot but not in sight of the A31 this delightful countryside walk, ideal for all the family and mostly good underfoot, takes you along well established paths and tracks, beside an attractive lake, across farm land and through woods.

1. Leave the pub and cross the road into Crow Lane walking until you reach a signed footpath and stile on the left, almost opposite Crow Arch Lane. Follow the field path across to the far stile and turn left onto the old rail line. Make your way along the track crossing the stile on the left and follow the path beside the lake, out onto the green and bear right making for the stile close to the farm building.
2. The fenced path follows the course of a stream before a stile allows access to a field. Ignore the path on the right but bear left up the field towards the fence, go through the gap and across to the stile. Climb onto the track following it up and round, past the

dwellings, into the lane and turn right.
3. Just before reaching the house take the path on the left along the edge of the wood. Upon reaching the lane cross over to join the path beside the boundary fence turning right. Just beyond the thatched dwelling turn left onto the gravel drive (the footpath is signed). Make a left turn at the next junction and keep walking until you eventually reach the lane. Cross over to the stile, then head for the stile at the bottom of the field and turn left keeping to the fenced path. After another stile cross the plank bridge into the field and make your way across to the stile and back to the pub on the far side.

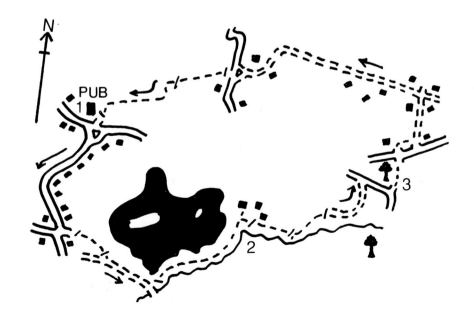

The Old Mill Inn, Holbury

Peacefully nestling in a valley close to Fawley, but seemingly miles from civilization, is the very picturesque Old Mill Inn. Originally a thatched miller's cottage, parts of the building date back to the 12th century and are reputedly haunted. Exploring the interesting bare brick walled interior one finds high and low beamed ceilings, discreet alcoves, cosy corners and a couch in front of a large inglenook fireplace where a warm fire burns in winter. There is a separate attractive restaurant and a room set aside for children who even have their own menu chalked on a large blackboard. Alfresco diners can sit in the pretty gardens where a watchful eye can be kept on the children having fun in the play area. Live music is featured every Tuesday and Sunday evening.

A managed freehouse the inn offers an interesting choice of real ales such as Ringwood's Old Thumper and 49er, Courage Best, Marston's Pedigree, Directors Bitter, Morland Old Speckled Hen and Websters Yorkshire Bitter.

Meals are served from 11 30 a.m. till 2 p.m. and from 7 p.m. till 10 p.m. Sunday 12 noon till 2 p.m. and 7.30 p.m. till 9.30 p.m. The selection, chalked daily on the blackboard could include breaded garlic mushrooms, ploughman's, hot tiger prawns with garlic and black pepper and a platter for two - consisting of potato skins, breaded mushrooms, chicken coujons and onion rings and reasonably priced main courses such as Barberry duck breast and orange sauce, chargrill steaks, a barbecue rack of ribs and surf and turf. Also plaice stuffed with prawns and mushrooms, pork curry and a homemade steak and kidney pie. There is a roast on Sunday.

Opening times Monday to Friday are from 11.30 a.m. till 3 p.m. and 6 p.m. till 11 p.m. Saturday 11 a.m. till 11 p.m. Sunday all day 12 noon till 10.30 p.m.

Children are welcome inside and dogs inside or out.

Telephone: (01703) 891137.

Not the easiest pub to find The Old Mill is signed from Lime Kiln Lane reached either from the roundabout at Hardley on the A326 or by turning into Park Lane from the Beaulieu to Fawley road.

Approx. distance of walk: 4 miles. OS Map No. 196 SU 427/041.

There is ample parking around the inn.

A slightly challenging but enjoyable walk across open heath, through woodland and Holbury Mill Pond - an area designated as a Countryside Heritage site in recognition of its nature conservation value. Nearby Exbury Gardens, open daily from 10 a.m. till 5.30 p.m, contains the world famous Rothschild collection of azaleas, rhododendrons and other rare trees and shrubs.

1. Leave the pub and walk back up the lane to the road turning right then immediately right into Park Lane. Although a fairly peaceful lane take care as there are no pavements. On the left are some attractive lakes and woods with various paths to explore which can offer an alternative route.
2. At the end of the lane cross over onto the signed bridleway opposite following it down to the gateway then fork left onto the blue-bell lined track through the trees (can be muddy). Pass through the gate and fork right past the dwelling and join the gravel track. Maintain your direction across open scrub, down to cross the stream then dogleg right up the rise and enter the Forest along the wide grass track.
3. Dip down to the stream, cross over and turn left following the path close to the inclosure. Further ahead cross the wooden bridge, turn right and then left over a smaller bridge making your way up the path ahead as it rises through the trees beside the inclosure. Just before reaching the wide gravel track turn right onto the smaller stone track, then fork right to reach the road by the half gate.
4. Walk straight across to the half gate opposite and follow the track ahead, past several tumuli before reaching a stile on the right leading into the nature conservation area. Climb into the field and cross to the gap on the far side (path signposted). Keep to the small stoney path walking down, round to the right and up to the stile. Maintain your direction across the heath, over another stile, past a pond on the left and over two more stiles. Ignore the first stile reached on the left but continue ahead to the second climbing over to join the little path through the wood at the end of which a stile allows access to the gravel track. Pass round the pylon to reach one last stile bringing you directly into the car park of the pub.

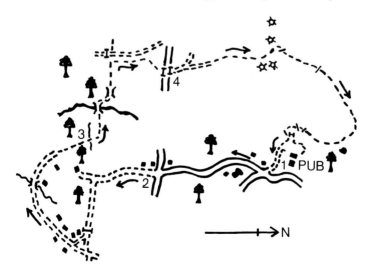

The Gun Inn, Keyhaven

Named after Colonel Hawker whose hunting gun claimed numerous victims and resided next door in "Hawker's Cottage" this 17th century white painted pub, situated close to the sea at Keyhaven, has in its time been a chapel and a mortuary. Fish nets adorn the outside whilst guns are displayed inside on the large brick fireplace housing a warm open fire in winter. Many nautical items and brightly shining copper and brass items adorn the walls whilst furnishings consist of comfortable red pew seating, farmhouse tables and chairs.

The well stocked bar of this Whitbread partnership offers five real ales which include Morland Old Speckled Hen, Flowers Original, Boddingtons Bitter, Marston's Pedigree plus a guest ale presently Old Smokey also Farmers Tipple scrumpy cider and 75 single malt whiskeys.

Popular with diners good food is served from 12 noon till 2.30 p.m. and 6 p.m. till 9.30 p.m. Those just requiring a snack can choose a ploughman's, baked potatoes, soup, sandwiches or garlic bread topped with cheese or prawns. But for those wanting something more substantial there is braised steak, cottage pie and locally made honey roast Cumberland sausages. Fish lovers can choose between seafood crepes - white fish, prawns and mushrooms in a white wine sauce glazed with cheese, seafood salad which includes green lip mussels, smoked mackerel, fisherman's pie, seafood cocktail and dressed crab whilst vegetarians can opt for cheese satay with peanut butter, garlic mushrooms and a dish such as vegetable lasagne. Heading the list of traditional puddings are spotted dick, treacle pudding and toffee apple and pecan pie. There is also a separate menu for children.

Weekday opening times are from 11 a.m. till 3 p.m and 6 p.m. till 11 p.m. Sunday 12 noon till 3 p.m. and 7 p.m. till 10 30 p.m.

Children are welcome and there is no objection to dogs on a lead.

Telephone: (01590) 642391.

Keyhaven is signed from the A337 at Everton.

Approx. distance of walk: 3½ miles. OS Map No. 196 SZ 304/915.

Park at the pub or in the 'pay and display' car park opposite

A very enjoyable and often bracing, scenic walk at first inland across farm land returning past Sturt Pond—a haven for wild birds, and along an attractive coastal path affording beautiful views across The Solent.

1. From the pub turn left, cross the road turning right into Lymore Lane when you reach the war memorial. Follow it round to the left, past the dwellings and between fields soon arriving at the signed footpath on the right. Proceed down this metalled farm road until it bears right at which point take the short track on the left leading to the stile, climb into the field walking across on the well trodden path to reach the lane on the far side then turn left.

2. In just a few steps enter the field on the left and bear right across to the far side. Turn right into the lane shortly to enter the field on the left (path signposted), walk to the fingerpost on the far side and turn left. Enjoy the views as you head down to the track then turn right, enter the road and keep straight ahead turning left at the T junction. Upon reaching the road turn right, cross over and pick up the footpath beside the telephone kiosk signposted, Sturt Pond.

3. Cross the road and make your way over the expanse of grass, join the footpath and turn left. Although good underfoot parts of the path beside the pond can become waterlogged during high tides. When you reach the wooden bridge either cross to the raised path on the shingle and stone breakwater returning to the footpath over the next bridge or keep to the path beside the waterway. For a longer more energetic walk you can even walk the entire length of the spit to Hurst Castle and return on the ferry, weather and tides permitting. The boat operates from April to the end of October and leaves every half hour from 10.30 a.m. onwards, last boat is at 4.15 p.m. Current charges are for adults are £1.50 and £1 for children. Follow the roadway round to the kissing gate, pass through onto the raised coastal path turning left when you reach the side track leading to the pub.

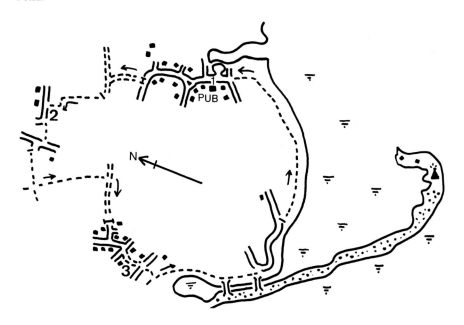

Red Shoot Inn, Linwood

Scatter rugs on the bare boarded floor and an interesting mix of furniture which includes heavy carved wooden settles, pews, carver chairs and solid refractory tables all add to the atmosphere of this very popular Forest pub. Paintings are displayed on the red painted walls of the open plan bar and a piano stands beside the brick fireplace where a warm log fire burns on cold winter days. A raised area of the bar is set aside for family dining and there are seats on the sunny front terrace.

This well managed Wadworth pub offers an interesting choice of real ales which include their 6X and I.P.A., Farmers Glory, and two from the local Ringwood brewery Best Bitter and 49er.

Food is served between 12 noon and 2 p.m. all week and in the evening, Monday to Thursday from 6.30 p.m. till 9.30 p.m. (10 p.m Friday and Saturday). Sunday hot food till 2 p.m. cold up until 4 p.m. thereafter from 7 p.m. till 9 p.m. The set menu offers diners the choice of light bites such as soup, garlic bread, jacket potatoes, ploughman's and sandwiches with interesting fillings like Stilton and walnut. More hearty meals include a brace of speciality sausages, chilli, lasagne and daily vegetarian specials plus two specialities, fresh fish in beer batter and sizzling steaks. Moules marinere, homemade steak and ale pie, turkey curry, roast pheasant in honey and rosemary gravy and spare ribs are all dishes that might feature on the specials board.

Monday till Saturday the inn is open all day from 11 a.m. till 11 p.m. (closed between 3 p.m. and 6 p.m in the winter). Sunday hours at present 12 noon till 10.30 p.m.

There is no accommodation in the pub but there is a camp site at the back.

Both well behaved dogs and children are welcome inside.

Telephone: (01425) 475792.

Dockens Water

Rockford Common

53

Walk No. 19

Linwood is best reached from the A338 Ringwood to Fordingbridge road at Ellingham signposted, Moyles Court.

Approx. distance of walk: 3½ miles. OS Map No. 195 SU 187/094.

Leave your car in the pub's car park or the lane at the front.

A very peaceful and enjoyable scenic, heath and Forest walk not too demanding but can be quite muddy in the winter.

1. From the pub walk back to the road and cross onto the green opposite. Swing left to pick up the wide track which rises steadily across boggy areas before narrowing and joining a cross track at the top. Turn right, and keeping fairly close to the inclosure on the right, walk to the corner at which point keep straight ahead up the rise continuing for a further several hundred yards, turning right onto the grass track.

2. Keep straight ahead at the cross track following the gravel drive towards the dwelling but just before reaching the entrance take the small footpath on the right behind the copse, across the heath then down through young birch trees to the valley and the stream at the bottom. Make your way to the far side and bear right, picking up the narrow path on the right which rises to a cross path. Keep straight ahead over the heath enjoying the lovely views before descending to the road.

3. Walk straight across onto the wide track, cross the bridge over Dockens Water and proceed ahead up onto the heath. Keep straight ahead at the cross track maintaining direction until you reach a wide grass centered gravel track then turn right.

4. Pass between the small wood and the trig. point and walk for a further quarter of a mile when you will reach a fairly wide track on the left leading to a circular brick structure at this point look for a narrow path on the right heading down the heath and follow it south turning left when you reach a cross path. Look to the right and make your way down to the wooden bridge and again cross Dockens Water into the field. Keep straight ahead eventually reaching the stile, exit into the lane and head uphill to the pub.

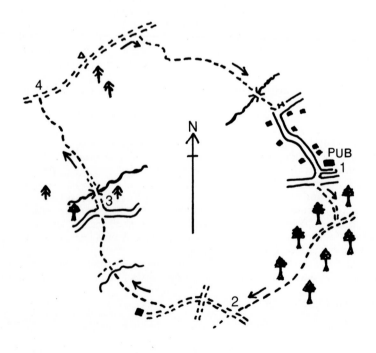

High Corner Inn, Linwood

Built originally as a farmhouse in the 17th century the very popular High Corner Inn is remotely situated in the heart of the Forest down a gravel track. Several cosy family rooms, one devoted solely to Lego, radiate from the main dark wood bar which has an interesting collection of bank notes pinned to the low ceiling beams. A piano stands beside the large fireplace where a warm log fire burns in winter. There is a second bar down a flight of steps, a restaurant, a function room, outside terrace, a beer garden and an adventure play ground for children even a squash court. Barbecues and jazz evenings are a feature of the summer months.

The inn is a freehouse run by the same family for many years. Three real ales presently available are Boddingtons Bitter, Wadworth 6X and King Alfreds Hampshire Bitter.

Food served from 12 noon till 2 p.m. and 7 p.m. till 10 p.m. has something to suit all tastes including children. From the printed menu one can just choose a snack such as sandwiches, ploughman's and platters also fresh soup, local game paté and melting Brie slices with red currant. Recommendations of the house include half a roast lemon chicken, corn beef fritters with grilled bacon and tomatoes and tagliatelli. Sound favourites on the menu include homemade beef kidney and mushroom pie and venison, bacon and stout pie, a mini grill and the larger 'High Corner' grill. Vegetarians have a good choice ranging from a creamed vegetable bake to pancakes filled with crispy vegetables and mushrooms. The specials board might include Cantonese style chicken, grilled plaice with pickled samphire. High teas are served in the afternoon.

Opening times are from 11 a.m. till 3 p.m. (2.30 p.m. winter) and 6 p.m. till 11 p.m. (7 p.m. till 10.30 p.m. winter). All day Saturday from 11 a.m. till 11 p.m. and Sunday from 12 noon to 10.30 p.m.

Telephone: (01425) 473973.

Walk No. 20

Not the easiest pub to find. The best route is to leave the A338 Ringwood to Fordingbridge road at Ellingham and follow the sign to Moyles Court, cross the ford and turn left. The High Corner Inn is signed down a gravel track about a mile beyond the Red Shoot Inn.

Approx. distance of walk: 4 miles. OS Map No. 195 SU 197/107.

Parking is not permitted on the track but there is ample space at the pub and a public car park further down the lane.

A most enjoyable scenic walk through woods, across open heath and farm land mostly on well surfaced tracks and dirt paths making it ideal for all the family.

1. From the pub turn left and continue down the track, past the cottages turning right at the bottom. Pass through the half gate, walk up to the second gate but do not enter the inclosure instead bear left, and a few steps further on turn right and join the path close to Dockens Water. In February 95 when I was here it was a ranging torrent but by August had all but dried to a few stagnant pools.

2. Upon reaching the cross track turn left, cross Splash Bridge and follow the sandy path up the heath soon to join the gravel track. Turn left and further ahead enter Hasley Inclosure forking left to reach the gate on the far side. Harvesting occasionally takes place in the Forest as happened here on my last visit. Should this still be the situation simply follow the track around the southern boundary.

3. On the far side pick up the dirt path and turn left walking down to the hamlet of Ogden's Purlieu. Turn left by the first dwelling, go across the bridge and turn right. (To shorten the walk or if desperate for a drink keep straight ahead up the track to the pub). Keep to the wide gravel track passing a few isolated dwellings until you reach 'Little Pointers Farm' then fork left, pass round the half wooden gate and follow the track up and round the boundary reaching a small hamlet. Walk past the dwellings and at the next bend turn left.

4. Cross the waymarked stile following the path to a second then keep straight ahead beside the fence, crossing three more stiles maintaining direction towards the field entrance opposite. Join the track at the top, pass through the waymarked gate to the left of the stables and follow the twisting path behind several properties eventually reaching a small bridge bringing you out into the car park of the pub.

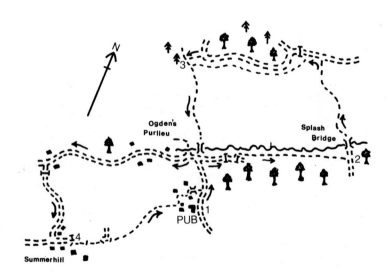

56

Splash Bridge

Ogden's Purlieu

Beaulieu Road Pub, Beaulieu Road, Lyndhurst

Overlooking open heath and sited close to the railway station, this very attractive pub is a popular venue for both locals and tourists alike. Warmed in winter by two open fires the bar areas have high ceilings adorned with a collection of baskets and hurdle fencing panels together with lots of interesting regalia and farm implements. The original stable block to the hotel is now a long, narrow attractive restaurant having comfortable seating one side and intimate wooden stalls the other. There is a large rear beer garden and an excellent play area for children.

The pub is a freehouse presently offering three real ales Thomas Hardy Country Bitter, Ringwood Best and Wadworth 6X.

Food is available every day from 11.30 a.m. till 2 p.m. (Sunday 12 noon till 2.30 p.m.) and 6 p.m. till 9.30 p.m. (Sunday 7 p.m. till 9 p.m.).

Amusingly written the bar menu, which includes meals for children, offers typical pub fayre of sandwiches, jacket potatoes, country ploughman's and lasagne plus a few specials such as tomato and basil soup and tuna and swordfish kebab. There is a little more choice in the restaurant like the 'Great Beaulieu Road Combo' for two - scampi, mushrooms, chicken wings and onion rings served with two dips followed by beef pie, honey roast hock of pork, whole pot roast chicken in a red wine and mushroom sauce, sirloin steak and a rack of ribs. Vegetarians can choose between creamy cauliflower cheese and traditional farmhouse broccoli and Stilton flan. 'Beaulieu Road' apple tart and sticky toffee pudding are just two tempting conclusions to your meal.

Opening times are from 11 a.m. till 3 p.m. and 6 p.m. till 11 p.m. Saturday 11 a.m. till 11 p.m. and Sunday from 12 noon till 10.30 p.m.

Families are welcome in the restaurant but no dogs. The hotel has 18 en suite rooms.

Telephone: (01703) 292342.

Pub is located on the B3056 Lyndhurst to Beaulieu road next to the station.

Approx. distance of walk: 4¼ miles. OS Map No. 196 SU 350/063.

Park at the pub or in the signed car park opposite. You can even arrive by train.

A most enjoyable easy walk across open heath and through heavily wooded inclosures. Mostly good underfoot it is an ideal walk for all the family.

1. Leave the pub turning left, cross the road and join the gravel track this side of the railway line. After passing the pony pens fork left following the track close to the fence. Ignore the bridge on the left but carry on along the sandy track which swings to the right, downhill and back towards a railway arch. Pass under and bear right across the grass heading for a gap in the woods where you join a track leading to a bridge. Keep straight ahead to a second bridge and across the grass turning left when you reach the dirt track.

2. Enter Matley Wood and about a hundred yards before reaching the half wooden gate fork left onto the narrow grass path walking down through the trees beside the camp site turning left onto the wide grass track at the

bottom. Head for the bridge then cross out into the road and turn left. Keep to the verge crossing over when you reach the entrance to Denny Wood Camp Site.

3. Stay on the main tarred road through the site then pass through the half wooden gate (beyond which point vehicles are not permitted) walking until you reach the dwelling on the left then turn left keeping to the path beside the boundary and straight ahead through the trees into the clearing beyond. Cross five bridges then take the path on the left forking left at the next junction. Cross two more bridges, ignoring the railway bridge on the right but keep to the track ahead, crossing one more bridge before turning right into the road over the bridge back to the pub.

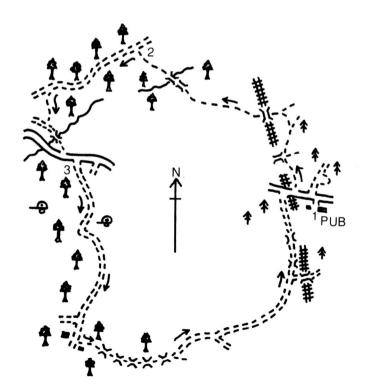

The Crown Stirrup, Lyndhurst

The interesting name of this ancient 15th century pub relates to Tudor times when the King and his entourage hunted in the Forest. Commoners could only hunt if their dogs were small enough to pass through the 'Verderers Stirrup' which can still be seen today hanging in the Verderers' Hall in Queen's House Lyndhurst, a former Royal Hunting Lodge.

Originally two small rooms the carpeted main bar has a low ceiling with some exposed beams, padded settles in the two small bay windows, and a brick fireplace housing a warm winter fire. A comfortable back room has rugs strewn on the bare stone floor, a mix of furniture, pew seating and interesting artifacts hanging from the beamed ceiling. There is a back patio and beer garden.

A Whitbread partnership the inn offers a choice of up to three real ales usually Flowers Original, Wadworth 6X and Boddingtons Bitter.

Food is served every day from 12 noon till 2 p.m. and 6 p.m. till 9.30 p.m. (Sunday 7 p.m. till 9 p.m). The printed menu, supplemented by daily specials such as game soup, and duck breast in a spicy sauce, lists Louisiana Cajun prawns, a platter of crudities and poachers lunch followed by Labskaus - the pub's own very special corned beef hash with a difference, locally cooked ham and eggs, Mexican chilli chicken supreme and a fillet of pork 'Roma'. For vegetarians there are dishes like a nut roast with a Provencal sauce and mushroom stroganoff and for those just wanting a snack gargantuan baguettes. Meals are available for children.

Weekday opening times are from 11 a.m. till 2.30 p.m. (3 p.m. summer) and 6 p.m. till 10 30. p.m (11 p.m. summer).

There is no objection to well behaved children and dogs.

Telephone: (01703) 282272.

Park Ground Inclosure, Lyndhurst

Walk No. 22

Pub located a mile south of Lyndhurst on the A337.

Approx. distance of walk: 3½ miles. OS Map No. 196 SU 302/073.

Park at the pub or at the top of the hill in the lay-by on the right.

A very enjoyable walk through densely wooded Forest. As there are no waymarks to guide you and numerous paths to follow it is important to pay special attention to the directions.

1. Turn left from the pub walk up the hill crossing over when you reach the Forest gate. Walk up the gravel drive branching left onto the path just before reaching the entrance to Coxlease School. Cross a clearing and a ditch before re-entering woodland. Maintain direction over a small bridge walking until you reach a gravel track. Keep straight ahead, round the bend and almost opposite a gate leave the track and join the path into the woods on the left.
2. Follow the winding path through the trees until you reach the wire fence of the inclosure then turn left. From here simply maintain direction diverting round the occasional fallen tree but always keeping close to the inclosure eventually reaching the track leading to New Park at which point turn left and walk up to the road.
3. Carefully cross to the gate on the far side and keep straight ahead across the grass,

turning left just beyond the clump of trees into the wide area of grass. Further ahead bear right joining a deeply gullied track rising uphill past old wooden boundary posts on the left to a clearing at the top.
4. Turn left following the undulating grass track downhill through the trees (diverting to the right of the fallen tree if still in place). Further ahead the path is better defined gently descending towards a ditch but well before reaching it look for a small cross track and turn right. Upon reaching a shallow ditch and open grass area bear right up through the trees to reach a clearing at the top.
5. Turn left and when you reach the car park, cross to the wooden gate and enter the inclosure opposite. Make a left turn upon reaching the wide cross track then left again at the next track leading to the gate finally turning right back to the pub.

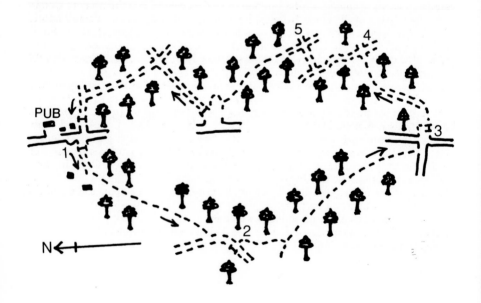

The Trusty Servant, Minstead

Minstead, a typical New Forest village, is well known for two reasons - one the unusual Inn sign depicting a servant with a pig's head originating, it is believed from Winchester College in the days when pupils had personal servants and the second its 12th century church. Inside there is a three-decker pulpit and some wooden galleries called 'parlour pews' which were reserved for the wealthy, one even has its own fireplace, whilst outside in the graveyard lies the body of Conan Doyle the creator of Sherlock Holmes. Rebuilt in 1901 the pub has a small public bar, a lounge and a very attractive candle lit restaurant seating up to 50. Some people though choose to sit in the rear garden or on the village green opposite.

Real ales on offer include two regulars, Hook Norton Best and Wadworth 6X plus a couple of guests changed weekly.

Good food is available everyday of the week between 12 noon and 2 p.m. and from 7 p.m. till 10 p.m. Popular bar favourites include ploughman's, sandwiches, filled Yorkshire puddings and potato skins with various toppings. There is a choice of pasta dishes, Murphy's steak and mushroom pie, a knuckle of lamb, various grills and fish dishes like halibut or tuna steaks with garlic or lemon butter. There are five vegetarian dishes which include garlic mushrooms and rice and a vegetable chilli, meals for children plus a roast on Sunday. The à la carte restaurant menu specializes in fresh fish and game.

From Monday to Friday the pub is open from 11 a.m. till 3.30 p.m and 6 p.m till 11 p.m. (all day Saturday and Sunday).

Children and dogs are both equally welcome.

Accommodation comprises 4 double and 3 single en suite rooms.

Telephone: (01703) 812137.

Walk No. 23

The small village of Minstead is signed from the south bound carriageway of the A31 also from the A35 between Cadnam and Lyndhurst.

Approx. distance of walk: 3 miles. OS Map No. 195 SU 281/111.

Park anywhere in the village or in the car park beside the pub.

One of my favourite walks through a most attractive part of the Forest along peaceful lanes and established paths. Although a little demanding when wet the walk is generally suitable for the whole family. Furzey Gardens, passed on route, occupies eight acres of delightful, informal gardens with something of interest all year round. Opening times are from 10 a.m. till 5 p.m. approximately. The current entrance fee is £1.50 for adults and 75p for children aged between 5 and 14. No dogs.

1. From the pub turn left back along the approach road and then immediately right into the lane signposted, London Minstead. In two hundred paces join the signed footpath on the left. Good underfoot with a spring display of primroses the attractive tree lined path rises steadily to a kissing gate and lane at the top. Turn left then left again at the junction.

2. Walk the length of the village, turn left at the road junction then right into the lane signposted, Furzey Gardens. Keep straight ahead across the brook and uphill turning left when you reach the gravel track leading to Furzey Gardens.

3. Walk past the dwellings following the path down through the trees forking right at the fingerpost. The path descends gradually through attractive woodland before reach

ing a board walk and plank bridge leading to a stile. Climb the path to the top and turn left, cross the stile, walk to the bottom of the field, over another stile and follow the narrow often slippery fenced path up to the stile, out into the lane turning right onto the signed bridleway.

4. Walk up the gravel track forking left and left again near the top. Pass in front of the dwelling and as you reach the road turn immediately left to join the signed bridleway. Walk to the lane at the bottom, turn right then left at the junction. Continue to the bottom of the lane, cross the brook turning right and almost immediately pass through the gate on the left to join the signed path up through the trees and past the church back down to the pub.

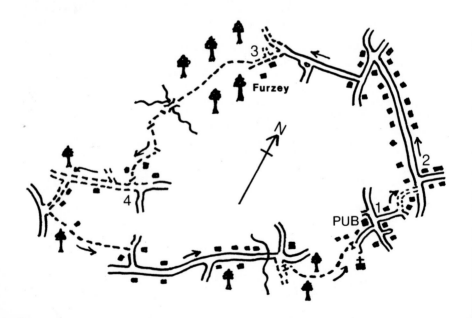

Minstead Church

The Lamb Inn, Nomansland

The lamb occupies an enviable position overlooking the village green straddling the border with Hampshire and Wiltshire. One can actually sit in Wiltshire watching cricket being played in Hampshire. Apparently at one time in the past closing times varied in each county so the locals simply moved from one part of the pub to the other. There are two bars overlooking the green having white painted and black wood walls adorned with antlers, a fox's head and other artifacts whilst the bar itself has an interesting thatched roof. There is a play area for children and picnic benches on the sunny front terrace.

The inn is a Whitbread house presently offering a choice of four well kept real ales. Wadworth 6X, Boddingtons Bitter and Fuller's London Pride plus Boddingtons Mild - a beer now disappearing from many pubs.

Generously portioned, good value bar food is served everyday from 12 noon till 2.30 p.m. and 6.30 p.m. till 9.30 p.m. (Sunday 7 p.m. till 9 p.m.). Apart from daily blackboard specials such as duck a l'orange, salmon en croute and nut roast Italienne the main printed menu lists a choice of starters, sandwiches, filled jacket potatoes, ploughman's plus the usual favourites like cottage pie and steak and ale pie. Quick and easy meals are served with chips, plus main course platters of chilli, curry of the day, a large mixed grill, roast chicken, lasagne and a Sunday roast. Vegetarians should be pleased to have a choice between leek and Caerphilly sausages, spinach and ricotta cheese cannelloni, Stilton and leek bake, mushrooms and nut fettuccine or a vegetable tikka masala. There are several reasonably priced meals for children which include an ice cream. For puddings take your pick from apple cherry and apricot pie, bread and butter pudding, apple and raspberry yogurt torte, treacle pudding and spotted dick.

Opening times at present are from 11 a.m. till 3 p.m and 6 p.m. till 11 p.m. Sunday 12 noon till 3 p.m. and 7 p.m. till 10.30 p.m.

Dogs and children are equally welcome both in the pub and garden.

Telephone: (01794) 390246.

Nomansland is signed in the far north of the Forest from both the B3079 and the B3078.

Park at the pub or in the lane opposite on the gravel area overlooking the green.

Approx. distance of walk: 2½ miles. OS Map No. 184 SU 253/173.

A short but very enjoyable walk through Bramshaw Wood.

1. From the parking area looking towards the pub turn left, cross the green and walk downhill to meet the tarred road at the bottom then continue along the road soon to turn left at the forest gate and enter Bramshaw Wood. Almost immediately bear right keeping straight ahead at the wide grass track and follow the path ahead, up through the trees until you reach a narrow track at which point turn left.

2. Keep to the main path which bears right dipping to a small stream after which fork left onto a narrow path between mature beech trees. Keep walking and where the path approaches a valley, but just before reaching the stream, take the well defined grass track on the right. Ignoring all side turnings proceed for some distance walking gently uphill to a cross track and turn left. To guide you there is a large oak tree and a heavy wooden post on the right. Follow this well defined route downhill between many mature beech trees, ignoring all side turnings (skirting tree debris if still in place) turning left when you eventually reach the road at Bramshaw.

3. Walk past the bus stop and just beyond the dip in the road make a left turn upon reaching the half wooden gate. The well defined track follows a course through the trees gradually veering right and eventually rising up to a car park. Go out into the lane and turn left walking the short distance back to the pub.

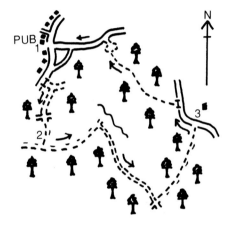

On the green looking north

The Royal Oak, North Gorley

Recently renovated and re-thatched this idyllically located, picturesque 17th century pub is set behind a majestic oak opposite a duck pond. New Forest ponies can often be seen standing close to the small fenced garden where a play area for children is located. The smaller, Cellar Bar has a low boarded ceiling, comfortably furnished with a fireplace at each end whilst the newly extended Cromwell Bar has a heavily beamed ceiling, part carpeted floor, wooden pew settles and a corner brick fireplace housing a warm wood burning stove. Down one step and you enter a family room and a cosy seating area originally the cellars but now doubles as a skittle alley. A back door leads out to the large attractive beer garden.

The well stocked bars offer a choice of five regularly changing real ales which presently are Draught Bass, Flowers Original, London Pride, Gales HSB and Ringwood Best.

Food is served every day between 12 noon and 2 p.m. from 6.30 p.m. till 9.30 p.m. and all day Sunday. The comprehensive food menu, supplemented by additional lunchtime snacks of jacket potatoes, traditional ploughman's and doorstep toasties offers the diner homemade soup, garlic mushrooms, homemade chicken liver pate, chicken satay and spicy BBQ pork ribs. There are steaks, a rack of lamb, a mixed grill, leek and potato mornay, garlic and herb tagliatelle and spinach bake for vegetarians plus old favourites such as steak and ale or steak and Stilton pie. Grilled Barberry duck breast or whole fresh plaice might feature on the specials board. Sweets range from homemade bread and butter pudding to Madeira cheese cake.

Weekday opening times are from 11 a.m. till 2.30 p.m. and 6 p.m. till 11 p.m. All day Saturday 11 a.m. till 11 p.m. and Sunday 12 noon till 10.30 p.m. (summer only).

Children are welcome in the family eating area and dogs inside or out.

Telephone: (01425) 652244.

Pub signed from the A338 between Ringwood and Fordingbridge.

Approx. distance of walk: 2¾ miles. OS Map No. 195 SU 161/119.

Park anywhere at the front.

Level at first and good underfoot the walk takes you across open farm land before reaching a track which rises steadily to the peaceful village of Hyde after which your route is across open scrub land before descending to the pub.

1. Leave the pub turning left and a few steps further on cross the stile on the left following the signed path to a second and into the field turning half right. Proceed across in the direction of the arrow towards the stile in the far hedge. Continue in the same direction heading for the yellow disc marking the gap in the hedge, pass through into the field and maintain direction across to the gap in the hedge, go out into the lane and turn left.

2. Round the bend, and at the next corner go over the stile into the field on the right. Keeping close to the hedge make your way through several gates finally turning right into the lane.

3. Walk round the bend, past the farm buildings and turn left onto the gravel track. Climb up past the dwellings and continue to follow the track ahead as it rises steeply up past the church, round to the entrance and up the drive.

4. Upon reaching the green at Hyde take the road on the right beside the school signposted, Ogdens. After passing some delightful thatched dwellings keep straight ahead at the crossroads, past more dwellings and into the clearing. Take the path on the right beside the hawthorn hedge walking until you eventually reach the track then cross the grass to the lane turning left. On the right there is a short track leading to an attractive gully which brings you straight back to the pub but although it is the nicest route to take if walking in the winter or during a spell of wet weather you would be better advised to keep to the lane as it can become extremely muddy.

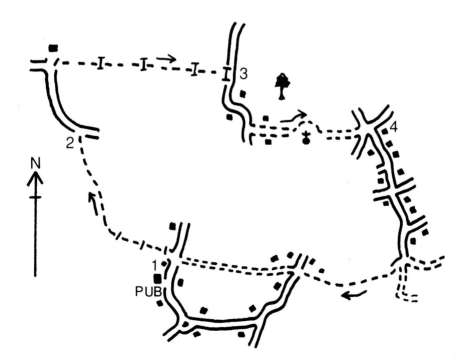

The Fleur de Lys, Pilley

One of the most attractive and oldest inns in the Forest The Fleur de Lys is a particular favourite of mine. In the entrance passage is a list of all the landlords since 1498 although beer is believed to have been sold here since 1096. Originally the inn was a pair of forester's cottages, the tree roots and fireplace opening (an old Forest tradition) can still be seen in the stone flagged entrance passage. The inn was described in Sir Arthur Conan Doyle's book "The White Company". One very attractive feature of the recently re-decorated, heavily beamed lounge bar is the enormous inglenook fireplace where hams were regularly smoked. There is a separate dining area and family room with a pretty rear garden.

The inn is a Whitbread partnership still serving real ale traditionally straight from the barrel at the back of the bar. Presently you can choose between Wadworth 6X, Brakspear Bitter, Morland Old Speckled Hen, Marston's Pedigree and Boddingtons Bitter.

A very good lunch menu is available daily between 12 noon and 2 p.m. (1.45 p.m. Sunday) with an afternoon menu served between 2.30 p.m. and 5.30 p.m. except Sunday. Evening meals are from 6.30 p.m. (Sunday 7 p.m.) till 9 p.m. Apart from the usual snacks of paté, ploughman's and cream of vegetable soup one could choose something more adventurous such as venison and wild boar sausages or perhaps green lip mussels whilst vegetarians might opt for a nut roast. Specials might include frogs legs or duck and pork pate followed by veal with white wine and asparagus, venison with juniper berries, roast pheasant, red snapper for two or black bream in oyster sauce.

During the week the inn is open all day from 11 a.m. till 11 p.m.

Children and dogs are both equally welcome.

Telephone: (01590) 672158.

Pilley is signed from the A337 between Lymington and Brockenhurst.

Approx. distance of walk: 5¼ miles. OS Map No. 196 SZ 329/983.

Park in the car park at the pub, in the gravel lay-by or opposite in the close.

One of my favourite walks which guides you along attractive bridleways, across open Forest and farm land and through Roydon Woods crossing The Lymington River. It is generally good underfoot ideal for most times of the year. Nearby Spinners Botanical Gardens feature azaleas, rhododendrons, camellias, magnolias and rare plants. Open April to August (except Mondays) 2 p.m. till 7 p.m.

1. Leave the pub turning right then left into Church Lane. Proceed down this very peaceful lane turning right onto the signed bridleway after passing Slade Farm. Good underfoot the grass centered track, rich in bluebells and other wild flowers passes between attractive farm land before reaching a gate at which point it bears left narrowing to a path passing through lovely woodland leading to a gate.
2. Enter the Forest and bear left following the well trodden path which runs parallel

with the inclosure, a good place in June to see early spotted orchids. Further ahead the path veers to the right around a hedged field and farm buildings, past a lily pond and a lone house on the left. Continue walking and a little further on look for a small ill defined path on the left which crosses diagonally to a wooden gate. Pass through onto the signed bridleway and follow the wide track up to the house and round to the left turning right upon reaching the track.
3. A few paces further on take the track on

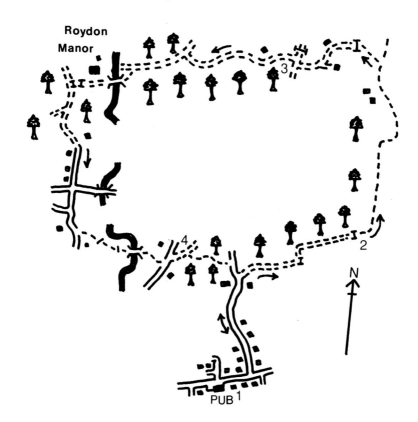

the left and enter Roydon Woods Nature Reserve. Good underfoot the track meanders its way through an attractive, broad-leafed bluebell wood. At the finger-post turn left walking gently downhill towards the river. Cross the bridge and keep to the track opposite passing Roydon Manor on the left, exit through the metal gates and turn left. The track soon becomes metalled passing some attractive Forest cottages before reaching the cross roads. Keep straight ahead into Roydon Lane, over the stream walking until you reach the finger-post on the left (opposite Tidebrook Lodge). Cross the stile into the field and keep to the

well trodden path heading for the stile opposite. Climb into the field walking round beside the fence to the stile then make your way across to the bridge and follow the path through the trees, out into the lane and turn left.

4. Walk up the hill turning right into the gravel drive leading to Rodleaze Rough Nurseries. Further up take the signed footpath on the right. Dotted with many wild flowers the attractive, undulating path winds its way through dense woodland eventually reaching the lane. Turn right then right again at the T junction back to the pub.

Lily pond passed early in the walk

The Lymington River

The London Tavern, Poulner

Once sited beside the main London road progressive road building has eventually left The London Tavern isolated in a quiet lane leading to Linford Bottom. This delightful village local, originally shops, is resplendent all summer long with colourful hanging baskets and window boxes. A single timber prop supports the high ceiling in the main panelled bar which boasts a large open fireplace housing a warm log fire. Furnishings consist of padded window settles, stools and tables whilst various nautical items and a collection of cigarette lighters are displayed in wall cabinets. Beyond this room is a new comfortably furnished family room completed in 1995. There is seating at the front and in the rear beer garden where there is a chalet and small play area for children.

The inn is a Whitbread tenancy offering a changing selection of five real ales. Typically there is Greene King Abbot Ale, Ringwood Best, Flowers Original, London Pride and Castle Eden.

Bar food is limited to jacket potatoes, sandwiches, plain or toasted, rolls and ploughman's together with a selection of pot meals like chicken tikka masala, tuna bake, meat balls in tomato sauce plus chilli and beef roughan josh.

Opening times, Monday to Friday are from 11.30 a.m. till 4 p.m. and 5.30 p.m. till 11.p.m (Saturday all day and Sunday 12 noon till 3 p.m. and 7 p.m. till 10.30 p.m.).

Children are welcome inside the new family room up until 9.30 p.m. dogs in front bar only.

Telephone: (01425) 473819.

Pub situated in Linford Road. Leave the A31 at the Poulner exit heading west, pub is signed.

Approx. distance of walk: 3½ miles. OS Map No. 195 SU 165/063.

Parking is very limited in the lane at the front but there is a good car park at the rear.

A most enjoyable walk through Linford Bottom for the most part on good tracks and paths making it ideal for all the family. All bar the occasional muddy patch the going generally is good underfoot.

1. Turn right from the inn walking uphill, and ignoring the Poulner turning steadily climb the lane until you reach the turning on the left to Hangersley. A short way down this lane turn right into Burcombe Lane, and after bearing left towards a dwelling join the signed footpath on the right. Walk down to the stile, cross into the field and continue downhill on the fenced path. Cross the plank bridge and stile and proceed to the stile on the far side, go over the stream and turn immediately left.
2. Keeping close to the stream follow the path over a couple of crossing points before reaching the track. Turn right and right again onto the Forest road then take the track on the left, cross the bridge and turn right onto the path across Linford Green to join the metalled road on the far side then turn left.
3. Walk to the top of the hill, turn left and then first right. Cross the brook and continue down the lane turning right at the

bottom in front of a house named Forest Acre then turn right and just before the letter box go up the track on the left. Walk round the house at the top and, keeping to the boundary, follow the path through the trees, across the drive and through the metal gate ahead walking down the track to the lane at the bottom, a route you will recognize if you have already completed the walk from The Alice Lisle.
4. Turn left and almost immediately cross the stile into the field on the right. Walk down to the stile at the bottom, cross the bridge and head up to the stile opposite then follow the narrow path up to the lane at the top, turn right then left onto the signed bridleway. Ignore the footpath to the left but continue ahead onto the narrow path which drops fairly steeply through a holly glade. Turn right at the bottom, pass through the gates and right again into the lane back to the pub.

Linford Brook

Linford Bottom

Alice Lisle Inn, Rockford Green

Alice Lisle, the courageous lady after whom this popular Forest Inn is named, lived in nearby Moyles Court and was sadly beheaded in Winchester for giving refuge to a couple of survivors of Monmouth's 1685 rebellion. At her trial the notorious Judge Jeffreys overturned the jury's not guilty verdict and ordered that she be burnt at the stake but the sentence was commuted after a public appeal to James II. She was beheaded in Winchester and buried at Ellingham Church close to Rockford Green.

Very popular with families this welcoming inn has two large bars. One mostly occupied by locals and heated by a warm winter fire has a separate games area whilst the larger has a servery and sunny terrace. Outside there is a very large play area for children which includes a mini menagerie.

Owned by Gales of Horndean the well stocked bar carries the complete range of their ales plus guest beers during the year.

Generously portioned food is served in the summer from May through till October, Monday to Friday from 12 noon till 9.30 p.m, Saturday and Sunday until 2.15 p.m. and from 6 p.m. in the evening (4.15 p.m. on Sunday) Winter 12 noon till 2 p.m. and 6 p.m. till 9.30 p.m. Apart from several pub favourites which include cold platters, chicken curry, homemade steak and kidney pie and lasagne the main selection is chalked daily on the blackboard. Regularly featured is a rack of BBQ ribs served on large oval platter and a giant hock of ham.

From May through till October the inn is open all day from 11 a.m. till 11 p.m except at weekends. Winter time from 11 a.m. till 2.30 p.m. and 6 p.m. till 11 p.m.

Children in patio bar only. Dogs allowed inside but not in the garden.

Telephone: (01425) 474700.

Walk No. 28

Take the Moyles Court turning off the A338 just north of Ringwood at Blashford.

Approx. distance of walk: 3 miles. OS Map No. 195 SU 159/081.

The inn has its own large car park but there is parking space in the lane by the phone box.

A delightful walk, at first around Blashford Lakes with their associated wildlife and later through delightful woodland. All bar the occasional muddy patch the going is good underfoot making it an ideal all year round walk.

1. Leave the pub turning right, walk past the phone box and just beyond Ivy Lane go through the wooden gate on the right to join the Avon Valley Path. From the bridleway one is afforded lovely glimpses across the reservoir. Continue past the entrance to the lake keeping to the perimeter path until you reach the gravel track then turn right and in fifty paces rejoin the path through the kissing gate on the left. After passing the lake on the left and upon reaching the cross path turn left following the stream, skirting another lake before finally reaching the lane close to the ford.
2. Keep straight ahead on the lane signposted, Highwood walking past some very attractive cottages before turning left onto the short track leading to Linbrook Thatch. (Look for the footpath sign). A wide tree lined gully rises steadily to a gate. After passing through bear left and, upon reaching the cross track, proceed onto the narrow path ahead. Cross the track and follow the wider track through the trees, bearing left at the next cross track and then fork left.
3. Just before reaching the dwelling fork left towards the entrance to Chatley Wood House then bear left to pick up the attractive path down through a heavily wooded dell. Leave by the gate at the bottom, enter the lane and turn right. After passing some delightful dwellings reach the crossroads and turn right back to the pub.

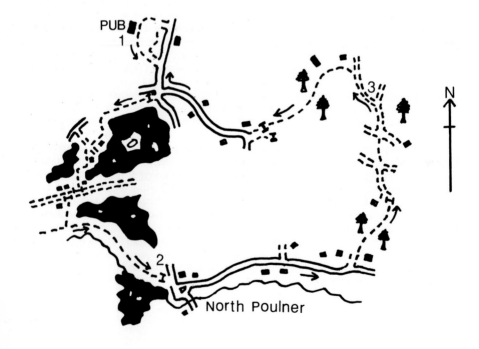

78

The Filley Inn, Setley

Previously known as "The Oddfellows Arms" this popular and reputedly haunted pub has two warm and welcoming, heavily beamed bars adorned with many interesting artifacts each with its own distinctive fireplace. Simple furnishings consist of farmhouse tables, chairs and pew seats whilst picnic benches are neatly positioned in the small rear garden. A new conservatory/restaurant is planned for 1996.

Well run by the owners, Lynn and Tony Bargrove this excellent freehouse offers a choice of four well conditioned real ales, Draught Bass, Wadworth 6X, and two Ringwood ales Old Thumper and Best Bitter. Also available is Caffrey's Irish Ale.

The set menu, available all week between 12 noon and 2 p.m. and from 7 p.m in the evening, which includes ploughman's, sandwiches, large rolls, garlic bread with a choice of topping and filled jacket potatoes, also lists various grills, homemade steak and mushroom pie, chicken coujons, omelettes and New Forest sausages. There are Filley favourites such as lasagne, chilli, deep fried potato skins with fillings and a choice of daily specials which might list homemade soup, smoked fish platter, fresh mushrooms in garlic, Jalapeno peppers and king prawns sauteed in garlic. Also available are specials for children, a Sunday roast and vegetarian meals like creamy vegetable Kiev, vegetable chilli, pasta shapes in a tomato and herb sauce and mushroom stroganoff. Steamed suet puddings served piping hot with cream, custard or ice cream are the sweet specialities of the pub.

Weekday openings times are from 11 a.m. till 2.30 p.m. and from 6 p.m. till 11 p.m.

Children are welcome inside the pub, dogs in the garden only.

Telephone: (01590) 623447.

Walk No. 29

Setley is located on the A337 between Brockenhurst and Lymington.

Approx. distance of walk: 3 miles. OS Map No. 196 SU 303/004.

The pub has its own large car park but limited space can be found in the narrow lane just beyond the pub.

Very good underfoot this short but nevertheless very enjoyable walk is an ideal ramble for the whole family along leafy lanes and on bridleways through the peaceful Roydon Woods Nature Reserve. Also suitable for mountain bikers.

1. Leave the pub turning left and left again into the lane. Walk up to the cattle grid and pass through the gate to join the gravel track which eventually leads into Roydon Woods Nature Reserve. Extending to 750 acres the woods consist mainly of broad leaf trees but also areas of conifer, heath and small ponds. An information board gives more details. Proceed along this track until you eventually reach the bridleway then turn left.

2. This very attractive and undulating track descends gently through trees to a stream then rises steadily past bluebell woods before reaching the lane. Turn left and walk up to the main road.

3. Go straight across into the lane opposite passing some fine New Forest homes. After the cattle grid fork left though the trees, across to the roadside turning left back to the pub.

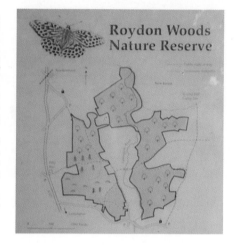

Roydon Woods
Nature Reserve

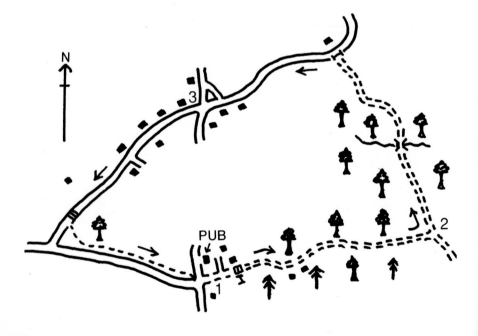

The Three Lions, Stuckton

Once a small country pub The Red Lion, owned and personally run by Mike and Jayne Womersley both experienced chefs, is first and foremost an attractive restaurant renowned for its high standards and excellent food even boasting 'Royal patronage'.

The bar is small mainly an area for pre-dinner drinks in front of the open fire but there are plenty of intimate seating areas especially in the recently extended dining area where light wood is much in evidence. Outside there is a small patio.

There are two real ales, Fuller's London Pride plus a guest such as Summer Lightning from the local Hop Back Brewery.

Food times are from 12 noon till 2 p.m. and 7 p.m. till 9.30 p.m. (closed Sunday evening and all day Monday). Although mostly à la carte the pub is quite happy just to provide a starter outside on the patio. All dishes are expertly prepared and cooked on the premises that even includes the bread. Typical specialities are "Billy Bi's" soup of mussels, or leek, potato and chervil soup, baby courgettes of game, salads of smoked chicken and bacon or goats cheese and pigeon and mushrooms stuffed with a fois gras pate, to be followed by fillet of beef with shallots in red wine and tarragon, escalope flambe with a Madeira sauce, roast duck with black currants or a spicy hot pot. There is a roast on Sunday and a choice of fresh local fish dishes such as fillet of hake in tomato and basil and lemon sole with a saffron sauce. Sweets range from lemon possets and creme brulee to hot chocolate pudding.

The pub is closed all day Monday and Sunday evening otherwise hours are from 12 noon till 3 p.m. and 7 p.m. till 11 p.m.

Well behaved children are welcome when dining with their parents. Dogs are permitted in the garden on a lead.

Telephone: (01425) 652489.

Walk No. 30

Stuckton is signed south east from Fordingbridge.

Approx. distance of walk: 2 miles. OS Map No. 195 SU 160/135.

The pub has its own large car park.

A short but nevertheless very enjoyable walk at first across farm land beside a brook returning along a peaceful lane and track.

1. From the pub turn left then left into the lane soon to turn right onto the gravel track leading to Brookfield Nursery. Cross the stile on the left and follow the fenced path, muddy at first but drier later as it rises through coppiced hazel trees to reach a stile. Cross into the field and head for the stile in the far fence then walk down to the stile opposite. Maintain your direction keeping close to Ditchend Brook, yomping a couple of ditches before eventually reaching the bridge.

2. Cross the brook and keep straight ahead to reach the stile on the left. Climb over

following the narrow path up to the stile then fork left in the direction of Godshill. The attractive path passes between fenced woodland and green fields before a stile allows access to the lane.

3. Turn left, cross the ford and walk up the hill forking left when you reach the gravel road. After passing a couple of dwellings the track narrows before reaching the lane. Turn left, past some attractive thatched dwellings returning downhill to the pub. Near the bottom on the right is an optional field path for a slightly shorter route back.

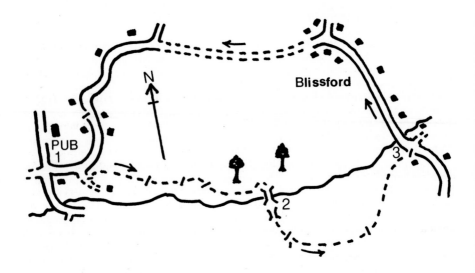

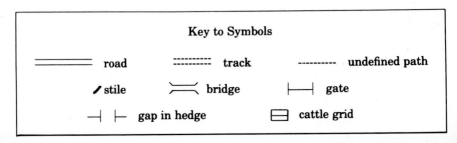

Key to Symbols

══════ road	┄┄┄ track	┄┄┄ undefined path
╱ stile	⤙ bridge	⊢⊣ gate
⊣ ⊢ gap in hedge	⊟ cattle grid	

The Plough Inn, Tiptoe

Originally a farm The Plough dates from 1630 evidence of which can be seen on a small section of wall behind a glass screen but in recent years has been comfortably refurbished and extended. Low wooden ceilings and a large open fireplace are features of the main L shaped bar whilst a small cosy side room is dominated by a large wooden dining table. At the back is a very attractive dining room with an interesting fireplace at one end and old farm implements hanging from the high pitched wooden ceiling. There is a safe, fully fenced play area, patio and garden also an adult beer garden away from children.

This well managed Whitbread house has five well conditioned real ales to offer imbibers namely London Pride, Boddingtons Bitter, Flowers Original, Castle Eden and Fuggles Imperial.

Food is served from 12 noon till 2 p.m. and 7 p.m. till 9 p.m. Posted on the blackboard the list includes cheesy garlic bread, pate or whitebait followed by perennial favourites such as a homemade chilli, lasagne, steak and ale pie or steak and kidney pudding plus a good selection of vegetarian meals like vegetable lasagne, vegetable Kiev, pineapple and mushroom balti, mild mushroom curry and a vegetable bake. There are lite bites such as peppered steak in pitta bread, sandwiches and ploughman's, several puddings for the sweet toothed and a menu for children. On summer afternoons tea is served from 3 p.m.

The inn is presently open all week from 11 a.m. till 11 p.m. and Sunday from 12 noon till 10.30 p.m.

Children are welcome but only in the restaurant whilst well controlled dogs are permitted in the bar and garden.

Telephone: (01425) 610185.

Walk No. 31

Pub sited on the B3055 east from the A35.

Approx. distance of walk: 3¼ miles. OS Map No. 195 SU 258/972.

The pub has its own very large car park.

An enjoyable mostly level walk, good underfoot on peaceful country lanes and gravel tracks entering open Forest for part of the way.

1. Cross over the road and turn left carefully walking along this busy country road for a short distance crossing back into Wootton Road signposted, Wootton and Tiptoe. A short way ahead turn right into Northover Lane. Proceed along this gravel track to the end and pick up the narrow path, walk round to the stile, into the field and bear left across to the gate, up the drive and out into the lane turning left.

2. Keep straight ahead at the crossroads into the dip then up the rise, through the gate onto the Forest and turn left. Keep walking until you reach the end of the gravel track then maintain your direction across the scrub and grass all the time keeping fairly close to the property boundaries on the left. After a while look for a metal gate with a built in stile at which point cross over onto the track and walk up to the road.

3. Go straight ahead into the tarred lane opposite, which soon deteriorates to a gravel track, walking until you reach the right-hand bend at which point cross the stile and follow the signed path round the field to the stile. Walk down the gully into the wooded valley, cross the bridge and follow the well beaten path up the field to the metal gate. Keep to the fenced path, pass through a second gate and finally exit through a third before reaching the farm shop and the road. Cross over and turn left carefully walking the short distance back to the pub.

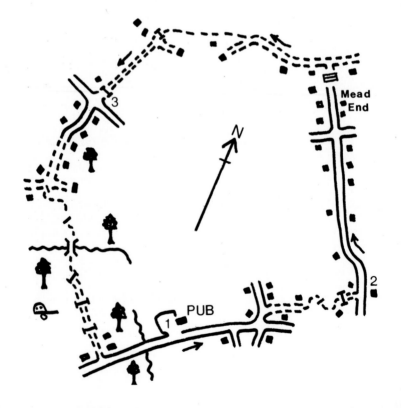

84

The Compass Inn, Winsor

On the edge of the Forest find The Compass Inn and you have found a real welcoming country local. Reputedly haunted this unpretentious pub is thought to be about 400 years old. The public bar has a pool table and dartboard whilst the lounge, divided by an open wooden screen to separate the family area has a low beamed ceiling and warm winter fire in a raised grate. There are swings in the rear beer garden.

Real ale lovers have a choice of eight well kept beers which presently include Flowers Original, Morland Old Speckled Hen, Ringwood Best, London Pride, Wadworth 6X, Boddingtons Bitter and Strong Country Bitter.

Typical pub grub, chalked daily on the blackboard and available between 12.30 p.m. and 2 p.m. and from 7.30 p.m. till 9 p.m. includes assorted snacks of jacket potatoes, ploughman's and a good choice of reasonably priced sandwiches followed by main dishes of chicken Kiev, steak and kidney pudding, hickory smoked ribs and vegetarian meals like broccoli and cauliflower cheese. Puddings change daily but freshly baked carrot cake is usually available plus trifles and fruit pies.

Weekday opening times are from 12 noon till 3 p.m. and 6 p.m. till 11 p.m. with the new Sunday hours in operation.

Children are welcome in the family area and dogs in the public bar only. Telephone: (01703) 812237.

Walk No. 32

Pub can be reached from either the A31 or the A336 Cadnam to Totton road.

Approx. distance of walk: 2½ miles. OS Map No. 196 SU 318/144.

Park at the pub or in the small lay-by in Barrow Hill Road opposite where there is room for a couple of cars.

A short but very enjoyable ramble on well maintained and well marked footpaths through attractive bluebell woods and along peaceful country lanes.

1. Leave the pub and cross into the lane opposite walking up and past the nursery and dwellings until you reach the sharp left-hand bend at which point cross the stile to join the signed footpath on the right. The path, good underfoot passes through a small wood before reaching a stile beside the road.
2. Make your way to the stile opposite and follow the raised path running between the stream and the fenced wood. Cross the stream and when you reach the stile climb into the field keeping straight ahead close to the fence eventually reaching a pair of stiles. Go over the one on the right following the raised path between the fields and enter the woods opposite, turning left and then right over the stile. Often muddy the winding path passes through an attractive wood

before eventually reaching a track at which point turn right.
3. Upon reaching the gravel drive continue ahead walking down to the lane and across the road into the entrance of Tatchbury Mount Hospital. Walk past the buildings and up the drive ahead turning right onto the track when you reach the signed footpath. Pass through the half gate, turning right at the fingerpost walking down and along the track only as far as the fingerpost on the left.
4. Cross to the stile and enter the bluebell wood. On the far side climb the stile into the lane turning right then left at the crossroads keeping to the right-hand side until you reach the church then cross back to the footpath soon to reach the pub.

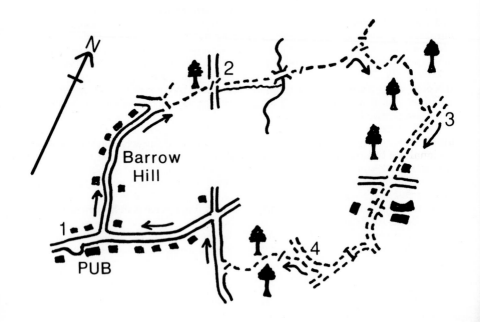

The Woodfalls Inn, Woodfalls

Woodfalls, the village from which this lovely Inn takes its name, lies just inside the Wiltshire border on the northern tip of the Forest. At one time known as 'The Bat & Ball' the present owner, Michael Elvis reverted to the original name after extensive refurbishment in 1990 resulting in the addition of a banqueting suite and en suite bedrooms. A winter log fire burns in the large open fireplace heating both a cosy seating area and the bar which is comfortably furnished with an assortment of solid, scrubbed pine tables and chairs. There is also an intimate dining room, a large sunny conservatory and tables and chairs on the front patio.

Michael keeps a watchful eye on the well stocked bar of this freehouse ensuring the constantly changing selection of real ales is served in perfect condition. A popular choice might include Ringwood Bitter, Courage Best, Directors Bitter, Gales HSB and Draught Bass.

Food served at The Woodfalls is to a very high standard acknowledged by many awards including the AA who voted The Woodfalls their "Premier Selected" regional Inn two successive years running. The bar menu offers tasty soup such as rosemary and courgette also salads, hot potatoes, ploughman's and the Woodfalls Casse Croute - a meal in itself. Hot platters include a hot sizzling full rack of pork in a rich spicy sauce and handmade faggots in a rich wine and herb sauce. Excellent fish dishes are chalked daily on the ceiling beam and might include pan fried fillet of sea bass with a fennel compote and flamed in Pernod, poached fillets of lemon sole with Vermouth and garden herb sauce, smoked medallions of monk fish in Cajun spices with a sweet mustard dressing and Cantonese prawns stir fried with egg noodles. Sweets range from apricot and ginger creme brulee to honey and rum bread pudding.

The inn is open everyday from 11 a.m. till 11 p.m, Sundays 12 noon till 10.30 p.m.

Families are welcome and there is no objection to dogs on a lead.

Overnight en suite accommodation.

Telephone: (01725) 513222.

Walk No. 33

Pub is on the B3080 signed from the A338 at Downton between Fordingbridge and Salisbury.

Approx. distance of walk: 3 miles. OS Map No. 184 SU 197/199.

Park in the rear car park, the road at the front or in the cul-de-sac at the side.

An enjoyable ramble at first down an old drove track with views across delightful countryside after which the walk continues along a peaceful lane before reaching The Avon Valley heading back up and across farm land to the village.

1. Turn left from the pub, and in 100 paces cross over into Lodge Drove. Continue past all the dwellings to the end of the gravel track then pass through the gate on the right following the old drove down through the trees keeping close to the boundary on the right. Cross the stile and keep straight ahead past the hazel trees (a very good spot to collect nuts in October) walking down towards the gate. Pass through to the drive turning right when you eventually reach Moot Lane.
2. Keep to the right-hand side along this peaceful lane joining the pavement after the bridge. After walking past a number of dwellings and side turnings look for The Avon Valley Path signposted to the right. Follow the gravel track up to the stile, into the field and straight ahead on the raised path. Enter a second field walking until you reach the stile then cross into the adjoining field bearing left up to the stile in the top hedge. Cross the track to the stile opposite and join the path which merges with a drive and leads to the lane. Turn right then right again at the junction, cross the road and return to the pub.

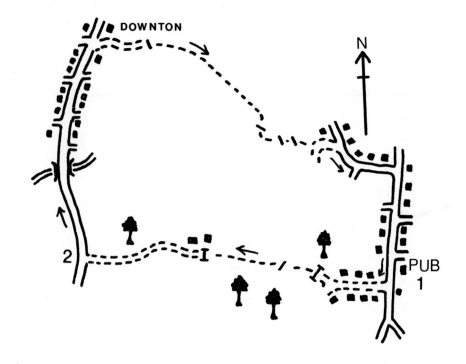

The sketch maps in this book are not necessarily to scale but have been drawn to show the maximum amount of detail.

View from the old drove

The old drove

The Horse & Groom, Woodgreen

The small village of Woodgreen is indeed fortunate to have such a splendid pub within its midst, voted by many to be one of the best in the Forest. Originally stables built over one hundred years ago, the cosy and totally original lounge bar has tables in front of the small open fire. Part wood panelled decor extends through an arch to a seating area with a piano and beyond to a new dining room which can seat up to 50. The pub also boasts a very comfortable and beautifully kept public bar also heated by a warm open fire in winter. There is a sunny rear garden with picnic benches and an aviary to amuse the children.

Personally run by the owners, Mike and Janet Whelan the well stocked bar presently offers real ale lovers the choice between Ringwood Best Bitter, Wadworth 6X plus a guest such as Pendragon Ale.

Excellent generously portioned and reasonably priced bar food, cooked fresh on the premises, is served every day between 12 noon and 2 p.m. and from 7 p.m. till 9.30 p.m. Following tasty homemade soups, garlic mushrooms and asparagus in a creamy white sauce there is grilled Avon trout, a 10 oz gammon steak or a 'Groom Grill' - steak, gammon, lamb chop, kidney, liver, fried egg, chips and peas. Vegetarians can choose between a vegetable lasagne or macaroni cheese. Pub favourites appearing regularly on the blackboards include tasty homemade steak and kidney pie and pudding both served with at least six vegetables also chicken ham and courgette pie, lamb and tomato in a herb sauce, leek mushroom and tomato quiche, ham and cheese crepes, ratatouille au gratin and New Forest pork and garlic sausages.

Families are welcome in the dining area and there is no objection to well controlled dogs in the bar.

Opening times are from 11 a.m. till 3 p.m. (3.30 p.m. Sunday) and 6 p.m. (7 p.m. Sunday) till 11 p.m.

Telephone: (01725) 510739.

Woodgreen is signposted at Breamore from the A338 Salisbury to Fordingbridge road.

Approx. distance of walk: 3¼ miles. OS Map No. 184 SU 171/177.

Park in the car park or the lay-by opposite.

A very enjoyable and peaceful walk for the most part through woodland inclosures. Apart from a few muddy areas the going is generally good underfoot ideal for all members of the family. Murals contained in the village hall depict local village life. Nearby is Breamore House a large Elizabethan house built in 1583, and fine Anglo Saxon 11th century church. The Countryside Museum shows examples of rural life whilst the 'Red Rover' stage coach is housed in the Carriage Museum. Open April till September (Tuesday, Thursday, Saturday and Sunday 2 p.m. till 5 30 p.m.).

1. Turn left from the pub keeping to the narrow lane soon to reach a stile on the left. Follow the signed footpath as it rises gently up and out into the lane at the top turning right. Descend the hill and turn left when you reach the signed footpath on the left, walk to the top and turn right. Head down beside the boundary hedge, cross the stream and follow the path up into the trees turning right at the top, walk round past the cemetery, along the track and out into the road.
2. Stride promptly across into Castle Hill pausing for a while at the view point before passing through the gate on the left into the inclosure. Turn right following the wide path through an attractive mix of deciduous and coniferous trees listening for the tap of a woodpecker. Keep to the main track which gradually swings to the left before meeting a wide cross track at which point turn left, walk up to the gate, cross the road and enter the plantation opposite.
3. Walk until you reach a cross track then turn left and fork right, keep straight ahead at the next cross track which descends through trees to merge with a track from the right. Continue down into the valley, cross the stream and bear left up the track ahead, round and out through the gate at the top onto the green.
4. Turn left walking down past the fenced cricket area on the right making for the seat on the far side of the lane. Climb the stile and follow the path down to a second stile finally reaching the pub.

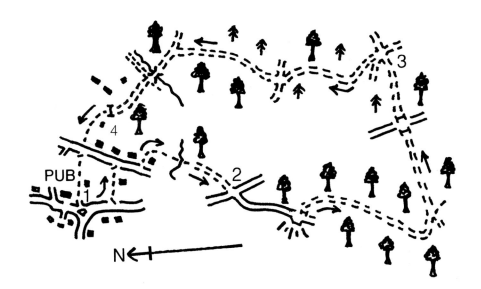

The Gamekeeper, Woodlands

Located in a peaceful lane The Gamekeeper, built around 1880 and previously known as The Royal Oak when it was owned by Strong & Co, has been recently refurbished but still maintains its traditional village pub feel. The main beamed bar, heated by a warm wood burning stove is decorated with bric-a-brac, tools and stuffed birds. There is a small dining room seating up to 20, a conservatory and a small garden.

Special events are regularly held which include quiz nights and auctions.

The inn is a freehouse well run by the owner Paul Hingston who took over in 1991. At present there are five real ales, Ruddles County and Ruddles Best, Wadworth 6X, Gales HSB and Ringwood 49er plus a sixth, Tanglefoot to be added shortly.

All the food is freshly prepared and cooked on the premises by two chefs. Starters include garlic mushrooms and whitebait followed by dishes like venison sausages, half a barbecue chicken, steak and Guinness pie, 'Gamekeepers' grill and various steak. The specials board offers more choice with a dish like rack of ribs with a hickory sauce. Lunch time set meals are proving popular as is the extensive homemade sweet list which includes lots of traditional sticky puddings, banoffee pie, liqueur cheese cakes and nutty treacle tart.

The inn is open all week from 11 a.m. till 11 p.m. Sunday 12 noon till 10.30 p.m.

Families are welcome in the dining room or the conservatory but dogs in the conservatory only on a lead.

Telephone: (01703) 293093.

Village signed south from the A336 Totton to Cadnam road.

Approx. distance of walk: 2¼ miles. OS Map No. 196 SU 324/119.

Park at the pub or in the lane at the front.

An easy level walk on wide grass and gravel tracks and a woodland path. Mostly good underfoot except during extremely wet weather; it is ideal walking for all the family.

1. Turn left from the pub walking up the lane until you reach the signed footpath on the left this side of the white thatched house. Follow the wide grass track past the farm buildings and up to the stile. Cross out into the lane and further on turn left onto the signed bridleway.

2. After two gates keep to the metalled track passing several dwellings until eventually you reach a signed footpath on the left. Climb the stile or push open the gate and follow the wide grass track ahead which soon narrows to an attractive woodland path winding its way through Fletchwood close to the stream. Pockets of primroses and bluebells form a colourful floral tapestry in springtime.

3. Reach the stile and cross into the field making your way straight ahead towards the fingerpost then arc right to the stile beside the gate. Walk up to the next gate and follow the track into the housing estate, out into the lane turning left back to the pub.

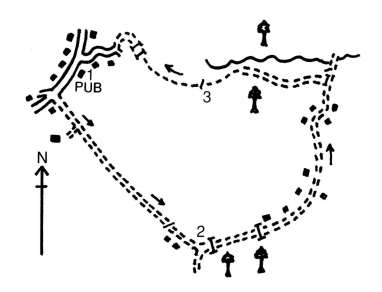

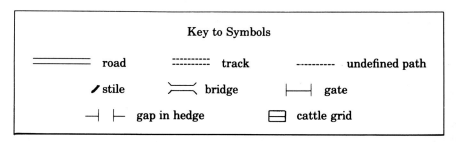

Key to Symbols

road   track   undefined path

stile   bridge   gate

gap in hedge   cattle grid

The Rising Sun, Wootton

Stained glass windows and doors are but one feature of the imposing exterior of this rebuilt Victorian pub bedecked in summer with a colourful floral display. The large bar has a Victorian decor featuring a cast iron open fireplace and comfortable furnishings which include an interesting assortment of solid wood tables. Outside there is an attractive covered patio, a beer garden and an excellent play area and pets corner for children. Facilities include disabled toilets and baby changing room.

The well stocked bar in this Whitbread tenancy includes a good choice of real ales such as Wadworth 6X, Flowers Original, Boddingtons Bitter and Castle Eden Ale.

Freshly prepared food is available all week which apart from light platters and ploughman's consists of specials like vegetable samosas, lamb balti, venison casserole in a white wine and Port sauce, West Country pork and Caribbean chicken - pieces of chicken breast in a creamy coconut and curry sauce. From the printed menu there are ten starters which include green Jalepeno peppers filled with cream cheese, savoury coated, deep fried and served with a salad garnish followed by traditional steak and kidney pie, chicken Dijonnaise, Lancashire lamb and leeks and chicken tikka masala. Vegetarian choices include cheese and tomato quiche, vegetable stroganoff and leek and mushroom pasta. Cream teas are served every day between 3 p.m. and 5.30 p.m.

The pub is open every day from 11 a.m. till 11 p.m. and Sunday from 12 noon till 10.30 p.m.

Dogs, horses and children are all welcome.

Overnight accommodation is available.

Telephone: (01425) 610360.

Pub located at Wootton on the B3058 signed from the A35 between Christchurch and Lyndhurst.

Approx. distance of walk: 3½ miles. OS Map No. 195 SZ 243/984.

There is a large car park at the pub and ample room in the lane at the side.

An enjoyable ramble across open Forest and through heavily wooded inclosures on paths and gravel tracks. Ideal for all the family there being no stiles.

1. From the pub turn right onto the B3055 Tiptoe road, cross to the grass opposite and turn right. Further on bear left picking up the track running along the centre of a wide grass strip. Walk for a good half mile before reaching wide grass areas either side of the track at which point turn left, pick up the gravel track and turn right following it down to the gate leading into Broadley Inclosure.
2. Almost immediately fork left onto the narrower of the two tracks, cross the bridge and continue walking through attractive woodland until you reach the wide gravel track. Make a left and then a right turn,

reach the gate, exit into the road and turn right.
3. Almost immediately cross onto the gravel track opposite and enter Wootton Coppice Inclosure. Bear right at the fork, and after crossing the small stream fork left onto the grassy track. Keep straight ahead at the cross track forking left at the next bend onto the gently rising grass track leading to a small gate. Pass through turning right and almost immediately cross the ditch, climb the tree roots on your left and enter the lane. After passing all the dwellings bear left across the grass to the pub which is now within sight.

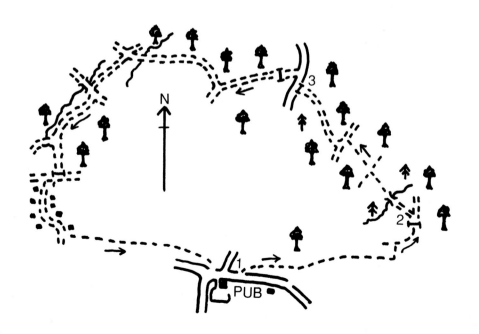

Horse trough on the green at Wootton